The RACE for ELIZABETH I's THRONE

'I wish not to live any longer, but desire to die'

Elizabeth I to Christophe de Harley,
Comte de Beaumont,
French Ambassador

The RACE for ELIZABETH I's THRONE

Rival Tudor Cousins

Beverley Adams

AN IMPRINT OF PEN & SWORD BOOKS LTD.
YORKSHIRE – PHILADELPHIA

First published in Great Britain in 2025 by
PEN AND SWORD HISTORY
An imprint of
Pen & Sword Books Ltd
Yorkshire – Philadelphia

ISBN 978 1 39903 733 4

A CIP catalogue record for this book is available from the British Library.

Typeset in Times New Roman 12/16 by
SJmagic DESIGN SERVICES, India.
Printed and bound in the UK by CPI Group (UK) Ltd.

The Publisher's authorised representative in the EU for product safety is Authorised Rep Compliance Ltd., Ground Floor, 71 Lower Baggot Street, Dublin D02 P593, Ireland.
www.arccompliance.com

For a complete list of Pen & Sword titles please contact
PEN & SWORD BOOKS LIMITED
George House, Units 12 & 13, Beevor Street, Off Pontefract Road,
Barnsley, South Yorkshire, S71 1HN, England
E-mail: enquiries@pen-and-sword.co.uk
Website: www.pen-and-sword.co.uk

or

PEN AND SWORD BOOKS
1950 Lawrence Rd, Havertown, PA 19083, USA
E-mail: uspen-and-sword@casematepublishers.com
Website: www.penandswordbooks.com

Contents

Acknowledgements

As always, I would like to thank my publisher Pen & Sword, especially Jonathan Wright, for allowing me the opportunity to write about such a fascinating subject. I would also like to thank Laura Hirst and Charlotte Mitchell for all their patience and support during the writing of this and all my previous books. Also, my thanks go to my editor Karyn Burnham for her hard work and patience during the editing process.

Thank you to my family, especially to my mum and dad who sadly passed away during the writing of this book. Thanks to Chris, Paul and Alison, to Mary, who sadly passed away during the editing phase of this book, Luke, Danielle and Faith, and to Kai and Kali – even though they are a little too young to appreciate the significance of the battle for succession! To my friends Marie Drelincourt, Lorraine Mawdsley, Kathryn Baxendale, Carol Worster, Pat Palmer and Gill Parker.

As always, a special mention and thank you to Emma Powell who as always has been unwavering in her support and encouragement. This book was written during a difficult time for me as my father passed away in February 2024 but Emma was by my side throughout, for which I will be forever grateful.

Finally, thank you to all the wonderful historians that have gone before me, their work is invaluable, you may not always agree with their stance but it is vital none the less.

List of Illustrations

Timeline of Events

18 January 1486	King Henry VII marries Elizabeth of York
20 September 1486	Birth of Prince Arthur Tudor
28 November 1489	Birth of Princess Margaret Tudor, Queen of Scotland
28 June 1491	Birth of King Henry VIII
18 March 1496	Birth of Princess Mary Tudor, Queen of France and Duchess of Suffolk
11 February 1503	Death of Queen Elizabeth of York, aged 37 at the Tower of London following the birth of her daughter who died just days following her birth
1503	King James IV of Scotland marries Margaret Tudor
22 April 1509	Henry VIII becomes King of England
11 June 1509	Henry VIII marries Katherine of Aragon
8 October 1515	Birth of Margaret Douglas at Harbottle Castle, England
18 February 1516	Birth of Queen Mary I
21 September 1516	Birth of Matthew Stewart, Earl of Lennox

17 January 1517	Birth of Henry Grey, Marquess of Dorset and Duke of Suffolk
16 July 1517	Birth of Frances Brandon at Hatfield, Herts
14 November 1532	King Henry VIII marries Anne Boleyn
1533	Frances Brandon marries Henry Grey
7 September 1533	Birth of Queen Elizabeth I
1534	First Act of Succession and the Act of Supremacy passed in Parliament
1536/7	Lady Jane Grey is born
19 May 1536	Anne Boleyn is executed at the Tower of London
30 May 1536	King Henry VIII marries Jane Seymour
June 1536	Second Act of Succession is passed in Parliament
12 October 1537	Birth of King Edward VI, his mother Jane Seymour dies shortly after the birth
6 January 1540	King Henry VIII marries Anne of Cleves, the marriage is dissolved six months later
28 July 1540	King Henry VIII marries Catherine Howard
25 August 1540	Lady Katherine Grey is born at Bradgate Park, Leicestershire
13 February 1542	Catherine Howard is executed at the Tower of London
8 December 1542	Birth of Mary, Queen of Scots, she succeeds to the Scottish throne at just six days old following the death of her father King James V

July 1543	Third Act of Succession is passed in Parliament
12 July 1543	King Henry VIII marries Katherine Parr
29 June 1544	Margaret Douglas marries Matthew Stewart, Earl of Lennox
20 April 1545	Lady Mary Grey is born at Bradgate Park, Leicestershire
1546	Birth of Henry Stuart, Lord Darnley
28 January 1547	Death of King Henry VIII, he is succeeded by his son King Edward VI
11 October 1551	Henry Grey is created Duke of Suffolk
6 July 1553	Death of King Edward VI, he is succeeded by his half-sister Queen Mary I following a failed nine day coup by Lady Jane Grey
1554	The Wyatt Rebellion takes place across England in protest against the marriage of Queen Mary to Philip II of Spain
12 February 1554	Lady Jane Grey is executed at the Tower of London, her husband Guildford Dudley was executed on Tower Hill
23 February 1554	Henry Grey, Duke of Suffolk is executed on Tower Hill
25 July 1554	Queen Mary I marries Philip II of Spain
May 1557	Birth of Charles Stuart
17 November 1558	Death of Queen Mary I, she is succeeded by her half-sister Queen Elizabeth I
20 November 1559	Frances Grey, Duchess of Suffolk dies
1560	Lady Katherine Grey married Edward Seymour, 1st Earl of Hertford

21 September 1561	Birth of Edward Seymour, Lord Beauchamp, at the Tower of London
1562/1563	Birth of Thomas Seymour at the Tower of London
29 July 1565	Marriage between Lord Darnley and Mary, Queen of Scots at Holyrood
19 June 1566	Birth of King James VI of Scotland (later King James I of England)
9–10 February 1567	Lord Darnley is murdered at Kirk o' Field, Edinburgh
26 January 1568	Lady Katherine Grey dies at Cockfield Hall, Suffolk
4 September 1571	Death of Matthew Stewart, Earl of Lennox at Stirling Castle
1574	Marriage between Charles Stuart and Elizabeth Cavendish
1575	Birth of Lady Arbella Stuart
7 March 1578	Death of Margaret Douglas, Countess of Lennox aged 62, she is buried in Westminster Abbey
20 April 1578	Lady Mary Grey dies in London
8 February 1587	Mary, Queen of Scots executed at Fotheringhay Castle
24 March 1603	Death of Queen Elizabeth I, she is succeeded by King James VI of Scotland who becomes King James I of England at which point the Stuart age in England begins

Introduction

The Fight for England's Throne

A History

When Queen Elizabeth II died on 8 September 2022 at Balmoral Castle in Scotland, the succession of her eldest child to the throne of the United Kingdom was seamless and unchallenged. But, unlike the accession of King Charles III, throughout England's history there have been many instances when the throne has been fiercely fought over – even if at times it seemed the heir was assured.

The throne of England has been contested and fought over as far back as 1066. When Edward the Confessor died childless in January 1066, four powerful men felt they had the legitimate right to be king. First, Harold Godwinson, Earl of Wessex. He was Edward's brother-in-law but had no direct blood ties to the king. Next came Harald Hardrada, King of Norway. He had no blood ties to England whatsoever, but felt the throne should be his by right because it had been promised to him, along with the Kingdom of Denmark, by Harthacnut, King of Denmark and brother-in-law of Edward the Confessor. Edgar Atheling was Edward's great-nephew, and as the last surviving Anglo-Saxon prince and member of the Royal House of Wessex, he had a pretty strong claim, that was until William, Duke of Normandy came along. William did have a family connection: Edward's mother Emma was William's great-aunt, he also based his claim on the fact that Edward had supposedly promised him the throne during an earlier visit to London. Initially, Harold Godwinson was crowned king on 6 January 1066 at Westminster Abbey, but that did nothing to deter Harald Hardrada or William from staking their claim. Harald attacked England's north-eastern coast whilst Harold moved his forces north to meet with the Scandinavian army at Stamford Bridge; Harald was killed early on and the English troops won the day. With the Norwegians and their allies soundly defeated, Harold made his way south, where he was to meet the great army of William of Normandy. To ensure the crown landed on his head, William invaded England, and on the morning of 14 October 1066, his army engaged with Harold and his troops in what we now know as the Battle of Hastings. It was a long and bloody battle that saw Harold killed; some say William killed him, some say he died after receiving an arrow through the eye. Either way, William was triumphant and became forever known as William the Conqueror, or William I.

William's fourth son, Henry I, ascended the throne in 1100, and in 1120, disaster struck when his only son drowned at sea in what is commonly known as the White Ship disaster. William Adelin, Henry's only legitimate son, had set sail from the northern coast of France along with many other nobles, including Henry's illegitimate children Matilda, Countess of Perche, and Richard of Lincoln, when tragedy struck off the Normandy coast near Barfleur. According to reports the wine had flowed abundantly among the crew and passengers, and the captain, Thomas FitzStephen, was asked to sail fast in order to overtake the king's ship, which had set sail before them, and reach England first. Unfortunately, the White Ship hit rocks on its port side shortly after setting sail, causing the vessel to capsize.

As panic set in, William, who had nearly managed to escape in a lifeboat, heard the cries of his half-sister Matilda and returned to save her. Sadly, all 300 passengers, save one, drowned that night, including William, the heir to the throne of England. This left Henry in a desperate situation, his only other legitimate child was his daughter Matilda. In the hope of having another son, he married again. Sadly, no children would be born to Henry and his second wife Adeliza of Louvain, and despite having twenty-five illegitimate children with eight different women, he was left without the one thing he desired most: a legitimate male heir. Left with no alternative, Henry had to name Matilda as his heir which plummeted England into a succession crisis.

When Henry I died in December 1135, civil war erupted; despite having previously sworn to accept Matilda as their queen, the nobles were not happy about being ruled by a woman, for it was not a woman's place to rule over men. Disgruntled, the nobility looked to Matilda's cousin, Stephen of Blois, as a possible ruler of England. Stephen had been brought up at Henry's court and was familiar with English customs, he was also well-liked by many of the country's aristocracy. After years of infighting Stephen won the throne, but only on the understanding that Matilda's son Henry would ascend after him.

Perhaps England's most infamous succession crisis took place in 1483, when Edward IV died unexpectedly at the age of 40. Edward had plenty of children, including two boys: Edward and Richard, but they were still only children at the time of their father's death. Edward was expected to assume the crown as Edward V, but his mother's family had other ideas. It was clear that Edward would need some form of regency until he came of age so his father added a codicil to his will to state that his wish was for his younger brother Richard, Duke of Gloucester (uncle to young Edward) should act as Lord Protector. His wife's family, the Woodvilles, decided to delay telling Richard of his brother's death in order to intercept Edward as he made his way from Ludlow to London. Richard, however, had loyal followers; as soon as he heard the news he made his way to the capital from his stronghold Middleham Castle in Yorkshire. Richard intercepted Edward and took him to the Tower of London. His younger brother, who had been in sanctuary with his mother and sisters, later joined him. The two princes were often seen playing in the grounds of the Tower, but over time they were seen less and less before disappearing from view altogether. Around this time news began to spread that Richard was going to seize the throne from his young nephew. On 8 June, the Bishop of Bath and Wells approached Richard with the news that his brother's marriage to the queen had been invalid because he had been precontracted to someone else; this meant the children of Edward IV and Elizabeth Woodville were illegitimate. Parliament begged Richard to take the crown, but many saw this as a plot to usurp the throne and steal the crown away from Edward. In order to shore up his plans, Richard had the *Titulus Regius* drawn up, a statute that stated his brother's marriage had been invalid and that Richard, therefore, was the rightful king of England. He ascended the throne on 26 June 1483 when he was crowned at Westminster Abbey. But what of the two princes? No one knows for certain where the two young brothers went. Many believed Richard had them murdered and buried within the Tower, others believe they managed to escape to the Continent; either way, Edward V ought to have followed his father onto the throne but instead he vanished forever.

It was not just medieval kingship that encountered problems. In 1689, the country was desperate to rid itself of the Catholic King James II and so looked to the Continent, where James's eldest daughter Princess Mary and her husband William ruled Holland. In June 1688 James II's son, James Francis Edward Stuart, was born to his second wife, Mary of Modena. The birth of the little boy sparked concern that the country was on the verge of returning to Catholicism at the expense of the Protestant Mary and her husband, who also happened to be the king's nephew. As the king's popularity plummeted the country's political elite realised new monarchs were needed and William of Orange was invited to come to England with an army to depose his uncle and father-in-law.

William agreed and arrived in England on 5 November 1688, at which time the disgruntled English army and navy decided to ditch their king and side with William. King James's reign was over and by December 1688, he fled England and headed into exile in France. Technically, James was the prisoner of William, but William did not want his father-in-law to suffer the punishment of a traitor and allowed him to leave the country. The fact that James had been deposed by his daughter's husband put Mary in a difficult position;

she was torn by the circumstances her father found himself in and by the duty she owed her husband. Mary eventually joined William in England and both were crowned at Westminster Abbey on 11 April 1689, becoming the country's only joint ruling couple. The Glorious Revolution saw the House of Orange take the throne without a drop of blood being shed.

As for James, a Convention Parliament was called to oversee the transfer of the crown from James to Mary II and William III (a similar parliament was held in Scotland for the transfer of its throne). The Parliament argued over whether James had abdicated or abandoned his throne given that he had fled the country. Different factions wanted different outcomes, some felt Mary should rule alone as queen, other felt William ought to rule as regent for James. But in the end it was decided by all that England was foremost a Protestant country and could therefore be ruled only by a Protestant monarch. James was a Roman Catholic so his reign had to come to an end. Naturally, there was some uneasiness over the prospect of Mary ruling alone given her gender, so it was agreed that she and William would rule jointly, although it was the king who held the regal power.

William and Mary ruled successfully but sadly their marriage produced no living children so when William died on 8 March 1702 (Mary had died in in December 1694), James II's younger daughter Anne became queen regnant of England. Anne oversaw the union of England and Scotland with the Acts of Union in 1707 and became the first monarch of Great Britain and Ireland. Anne married Prince George of Denmark in 1683 and gave birth to their son, Prince William, Duke of Gloucester, in July 1689; he sadly died aged 11, devastating his parents. Anne had seventeen pregnancies, with William being the only child to survive infancy; his death brought about a new succession crisis. The Stuart era ended with the death of Queen Anne in August 1714, as her great-great-great-grandfather James V of Scotland predicted 'it cam wi a lass, it'll gang wi a lass'.

There were several options open to the British government but they chose to ignore the many claimants who were Catholic as per the Act of Settlement of 1701, which barred all Catholics from claiming the throne, and therefore looked to the German states for their next king. The biggest claimant was Anne's half-brother James Stuart, who later became known as the Old Pretender, but he was overlooked due to his religion so Anne's second cousin, George of Hanover, whose grandmother was Elizabeth Stuart, daughter of James I, was invited to become King of Great Britain.

Supporters of James Stuart called themselves the Jacobites; they threatened the stability of George's reign by rebelling against foreign rule and by the notion that 'the Old Pretender' was a much better claimant. The Jacobite Rebellion spanned many years and James's son, Charles Edward Stuart, or Bonny Prince Charlie as he is better known, tried to regain the British throne for his father. After many pitched battles, the rebellion finally ended with the Battle of Culloden in Scotland, and so the Georgian period began.

The winning and keeping of a crown has never been easy, Richard III went into battle against Henry Tudor to keep his throne but failed and the new Tudor dynasty brought stability. But when Prince Arthur, the heir of Henry VII and his queen, Elizabeth of York, died in 1502, they had a second son, Henry, who took the crown; that Henry changed the face of England to ensure his crown was passed to his legitimate born son. Henry VIII desperately needed a son and heir and when his first wife, Katherine of Aragon, provided him with only a daughter, he decided to look elsewhere. He met and fell in love with Anne Boleyn, and over a period of years he strove to find a way of annulling his marriage with Katherine to marry Anne. In the end, he broke England away from Rome and made himself the Supreme Head of the Church of England. He married Anne Boleyn in the hope she could give him his much-coveted prince; sadly for her, she did not, and paid the price with her head. Henry did finally have a son with his third wife Jane Seymour, and that boy became Edward VI. Sadly, Edward died at the age of 15 and rather than name his half-sister, the Catholic

Mary, as his heir as their father had wished, he named his cousin, Lady Jane Grey, as queen. Mary had plenty of supporters who rallied to her cause and Jane only managed to reign for nine days. Mary was unable to produce her own heir despite being married to Philip of Spain – heartbreakingly, she experienced a phantom pregnancy; although displaying all the signs of being with child, the due date passed and it became apparent there would be no child. Mary was devastated. When it became a reality that she would not be able to have a child, she battled, like Elizabeth, over who should succeed her to the throne. Her cousin and dear friend, the Catholic Margaret Douglas, Countess of Lennox, was the queen's favourite choice but she was unable to get this through parliament and so declared her Protestant half-sister Elizabeth as her heir.

When Elizabeth I died childless in 1603, we find the country once again amid another succession crisis. She had decided not to marry and produce an heir of her own and had resolutely refused to name one during her reign, despite the persistent requests from her council. The question regarding the succession of the English crown went far beyond English shores. Spain, France and the Pope in Rome all had their preferred choices and they all held their breath as Elizabeth I lay on her deathbed. Would the succession crisis lead to civil war – or worse, a foreign invasion? There were many contenders throughout her reign, both male and female, Protestant and Catholic, but only one could reign supreme and when Elizabeth finally passed away in March 1603 there was just one name on her lips.

The Last Will and Testament of King Henry VIII

An Author's Note

The last will of Henry VIII has become one of English history's most contested and argued over documents. King Henry's final hours have been documented in John Foxe's *Acts and Monuments*, which was written during the reign of Elizabeth I, so while not contemporary, it is considered to be a well-trusted account. Foxe's account tells us that Henry had been sleeping for a couple of hours when he awoke to the realisation that his end was coming. He requested the presence of Archbishop Cranmer but it took time for him to make the journey from his home in Croydon to Westminster, given the frozen state of the roads. Foxe goes on to explain that by the time the archbishop had arrived, Henry could no longer speak and was drifting in and out of consciousness. The king managed to reach out a hand, at which point Cranmer knew there was no time for the crucifix or to administer communion, instead, he asked the king to put his trust in Jesus Christ and his faith in the Lord. Cranmer then asked Henry to give a sign that he had heard and understood what had been said to him. The king again reached out a hand, and with that final act, he died.

Henry VIII died on 28 January 1547 at Westminster Palace, London, leaving his 9-year-old son, Prince Edward, as his heir. However, in 1536 at the age of 45, Henry had been without a legitimate heir. He had two daughters, Mary and Elizabeth, but Henry wanted a male heir. He decided to pass the Act of Settlement 1536 which, confirmed the illegitimacy of his daughters and removed them completely from the line of succession. It also decreed that any child born of Jane Seymour, Henry's third wife – or indeed any future wife – would succeed him to the throne. But what if there were to be no more children born to Henry? The last thing the country needed was a realm left without an heir so the Act instructed that Henry had the right to name his own successor by the terms of his will. This was later confirmed in the Act of Succession 1544, even though by that time Prince Edward had been born, in 1537, and was the undisputed heir of his father the king. But other amendments were made, mainly that Mary and Elizabeth were reinstated to the succession but remained illegitimate and did not have the title of princess restored to them. Constitutionally, Henry's last will became a focal point of the Tudor reign, it was temporarily overlooked when Edward VI nominated his cousin Lady Jane Grey over his half-sister Mary, but beyond that, the line of succession did follow Henry's will because by the time Elizabeth died in 1603, the claimants stated had also passed away or been made illegitimate.

But why was the will so controversial? Henry made amendments to his will on 30 December 1546 but questions have been raised over whether it was valid and if it did actually contain Henry's final wishes. The will was drafted by Sir William Paget, a loyal secretary of Henry's, and it discusses Henry's wishes for his burial, which his children overlooked; it also discusses the distribution of the king's estate. But the bulk of the document is regarding the succession, and Henry lays out various scenarios; for example, if Edward dies without issue, then the crown would pass to Mary, and then her heirs; or Elizabeth, should Mary not produce an heir etc. It also names sixteen executors and members of the Privy Council that are to guide Edward until he reaches his majority at 18 years old, they are to keep the realm at peace and secure until Edward took power.

But there are conspiracies that surround the will. First, that there was a coup to remove certain members of the Regency Council, mainly Stephen Gardiner, Bishop of Winchester, and Thomas Howard, Duke of Norfolk, who incidentally would find himself in the Tower of London facing death at the time Henry died. There were two factions at court linked by religious belief, the Evangelicals and the Conservatives. Two of the major Evangelicals were Sir William Paget and Edward Seymour, Earl of Hertford. The accusation is that they amended the will to remove Stephen Gardiner and Thomas Howard, and also that they added further clauses between the December amendments and Henry's death in January which enabled them to take sole power; the Evangelicals wanted sole power so they could impose their own religious reforms on the country. The will was then stamped by Henry. This seems doubtful however, given that Gardiner was Paget's mentor and so was unlikely to have removed him. It is more likely that Henry asked for him to be removed as Gardiner had upset the king in some way. As for the Duke of Norfolk, he was removed given his brush with treason at the hands of his son, who decided to quarter his arms with those of the royal arms.

The second query is over whether or not the will was signed when it was dated, and whether it had then been subsequently amended after being signed. The will had been 'dry-stamped' using the king's cypher; in effect, Henry did not need to be there, so was it legal and binding? That does not seem to be the issue here though. In order for the document to be valid, it had to be registered by the end of December with the schedule of clerks instead. This did not happen until January, which undermines the legality of the will. It is hard to see how the will could have been amended after the event; there does not seem to be much room for anyone to add or amend any information.

We will never know for certain if the instructions given in the last will and testament are in fact the dying wishes of the king, but that document would be referred to again and again from the reign of Edward VI to Elizabeth I, and whether it was considered a legally binding document or not would depend on the religious persuasion of those concerned.

A transcript of Henry VIII's will can be found under Appendix One.

Chapter One

Who was Elizabeth I?

If you were to ask most people who the most popular or successful monarch in England's history was, many would say Queen Elizabeth II – and rightly so, but her namesake Elizabeth I ranks not far behind her. Like the late queen, Elizabeth Tudor became queen at just 25 and at birth was not considered a likely candidate for the throne. Unlike Elizabeth II, her Tudor counterpart did not marry and have children, but did prove that a woman could rule independently and successfully. She paved the way for later monarchs such as Queen Anne and Queen Victoria to take on the crown without fear that they would not be able to rule because of their gender; they also oversaw great shifts in the country's development.

Elizabeth Tudor was born on 7 September 1533 at Greenwich Palace, she was the younger daughter of Henry VIII and his second wife, Anne Boleyn. At the time of her birth, she supplanted her elder half-sister Mary by becoming the heir presumptive, and was to remain so until a male child was born. She was baptised on 10 September and sent to the royal nursery before being established with her own household. Much of Elizabeth's early life was spent away from court and when Henry had Anne executed on charges of treason, Elizabeth's life, at the age of just 2 and a half, looked uncertain. She suffered an immediate fall from grace, much like her elder half-sister Mary had just a few years before, and was subsequently placed within the household of her new half-brother, Prince Edward.

In 1537, King Henry became a father to a prince when his third wife, Jane Seymour, finally gave birth to the much anticipated and long-awaited son, Edward. His birth meant Elizabeth now sat third in line for the throne, after her new baby brother and half-sister Mary. Edward died without issue at the age of 15 and had initially named his cousin Lady Jane Grey as his heir, but she sat on the throne for just nine days (technically, it was thirteen if we count from the day of Edward's death but she is known to history as the nine-day queen). Jane's accession was not popular and Mary soon captured her throne, which she ascended in July 1553; she reigned for five years. Elizabeth, as a Protestant in a Catholic monarchy, was constantly under supervision and suspicion and considered illegitimate, because her father had declared her so. But when Mary died childless in November 1558, Elizabeth Tudor succeeded to the throne of England.

Elizabeth made her triumphal entrance into London the evening before her coronation at Westminster Abbey on 15 January 1559, the people were overjoyed to have a young queen on the throne. Behind all the pageantry and good wishes, however, they were concerned about the potential religious upheaval a new monarch might bring. Religion was the biggest and most immediate issue facing Elizabeth at the beginning of her reign. She had inherited a country that was part Catholic and part Protestant and she somehow, as the new queen, had to manage to establish a Church of England that sought compromises between Catholicism and Protestantism. Elizabeth's own religious stance has often been debated; outwardly, she was a Protestant, but she did retain some Catholic beliefs, including the worship of the crucifix, and she was keen to make changes that were sympathetic to Catholic beliefs. She managed to keep it on an even footing and declared to her people there was only one Jesus Christ and all the other disputes were merely 'trifles'. The people of England were happy to finally have some religious stability and embraced the new church.

Elizabeth was a very intelligent woman; she had been given an excellent standard of education by her father and was one determined to govern her way. Many believed that without a husband at her side there was no way she could rule successfully, so a petition for her to marry was drawn up by the House of Commons on the first day of Elizabeth's parliament, such was the pressing issue of her marriage. It was at this point that Elizabeth declared she had no intention of marrying. She had made a conscious choice not to marry and bear the next heir, choosing instead to rule alone and knowingly bring to an end the Tudor dynasty.

Her council, however, persisted and offered suitors for her to consider. But why did she refuse? She knew it was her duty to marry and produce an heir for the country. Firstly, if she did marry she would have to answer to her husband, and as queen she was not willing to lose that autonomy of not having to explain herself to anyone. Also, let us consider her parents' marriage. In the beginning, it was a true love story. Henry VIII had begged, pleaded, and even defied Rome to marry Elizabeth's mother Anne Boleyn. But in such a short space of time it turned sour, and Henry had his wife executed on charges of treason and incest. Surely, when Elizabeth learned of these details it must have horrified her. She was a small child when Anne was executed and probably had no memories of her mother. Her relationship with her father was rocky for a time, although the influence of his later wives helped repair that damage.

Finally, she had to consider the stability of the country. What would happen if she made the wrong choice? If she married a foreign prince and the marriage went sour, then it could risk a foreign invasion. On the other hand, if she married an Englishman, her choice could be perceived as favouritism and risk upsetting a number of her loyal noble families. It was a fine balancing act and it seems the easiest solution all round was to remain unmarried. A further angle to take into consideration was her close relationship with Robert Dudley. It was during the ongoing marriage discussions of 1559 that it became clear Elizabeth had strong feelings for Dudley and that he would be her choice of husband – the problem was, he was already married. The pair had been close friends since childhood and when Elizabeth became queen, he became a constant at her side. Dudley's wife Amy

Robsart was found dead at the foot of the stairs at her home, Cumnor Place in Oxfordshire. She had sent her servants away for the day to enjoy a local fair, and when they came back, they found Amy dead at the foot of the stairs. The cause of death was given as a broken neck and was ruled an accident, but that did not stop many people from suspecting Dudley of having arranged his wife's death. Did she fall, or was she pushed? People believed he had her killed so that he would be free to marry Elizabeth, but the irony is that Amy's death became the one thing that prevented that marriage from happening because the queen could never marry someone suspected of murder. However, Elizabeth took her time and did consider taking Dudley as her husband, regardless of the rumours, but her council made it clear they would not support her if she did. Elizabeth made Dudley the Earl of Leicester in 1564, and the pair remained the closest of friends until his death in 1588. Was this the reason she never married? If she could not marry her one true love, then she would not marry at all.

I think it is safe to say Elizabeth had issues with men. Her father executed her mother which must have had a lasting effect on her feelings towards her father. At the age of just 14, following the death of her father, Elizabeth went to live in the household of her stepmother, Katherine Parr. Five months after the death of Henry VIII, Katherine married Thomas Seymour, Baron Sudeley; he was power-hungry and hell bent on ingratiating himself with the royal family. Despite being uncle to King Edward and brother of Edward Seymour, the Lord Protector, he was on the fringes of the inner circle and felt he deserved much more. Katherine offered Elizabeth a maternal figure and they had always been close, but sadly, Seymour was far from the father figure Elizabeth needed. Elizabeth's governess, Kat Ashley, approached Katherine to advise her that Seymour had been coming to the princess's bedchamber to say good morning, wearing nothing but a nightshirt. He would chase her around the room, tickling her and slapping her backside while trying to kiss her on the lips. This behaviour confused Elizabeth so in a bid to avoid Seymour she tried to rise early and surround herself with her ladies in the hope it would deter him. Reports suggest he once ripped her gown into a thousand pieces. Katherine was pregnant at the time and dismissed Ashley's concerns, claiming it was only a bit of fun – in fact the queen would join her husband on a couple of occasions to allay any fears, but she soon grew suspicious and concerned at his reckless behaviour. Some accounts state that while walking in her gardens Katherine came upon Elizabeth and Seymour in an embrace. Elizabeth was dismissed from the household with a warning from Katherine that her good name was at risk; being the daughter of Anne Boleyn, Elizabeth had to work harder at retaining her unblemished reputation.

As Elizabeth was in the line of succession, she was not free to marry where she wished; any future husband would have to be agreed upon by the Privy Council so when Seymour began bombarding her with letters, Elizabeth refused to reply. Kat Ashley was fond of Seymour, so she entered into negotiations over a potential marriage with Elizabeth. She discussed Elizabeth's financial situation and land holding with him without her knowledge. Somehow, word reached the Privy Council that Seymour was plotting to marry Elizabeth so he was arrested on the orders of his brother, the Lord Protector, in January 1549. Elizabeth was questioned, along with her servants. Ashley told her interviewer about Seymour's visits to the princess's bedchamber and about the marriage negotiations, but she stated Elizabeth had no prior knowledge of these. Elizabeth consistently denied knowing what Seymour was planning and confirmed she had no intention of marrying him. The council believed Elizabeth and her servants, but a terrible fate awaited Seymour. He stood accused not only of trying to marry Elizabeth, but also of attempting to overthrow the Lord Protector, and that was an act of treason. The Act of Attainder was passed on 10 March 1549 by his nephew King Edward. Seymour was beheaded ten days later on Tower Hill.

It is easy to see why Elizabeth was wary of men; to her they were brutes who executed wives, and rogues who only wanted to marry her to better themselves. If she had not crossed paths with

Seymour maybe her views would have been different. These days, her experiences at his hands would be classed as grooming, and his behaviour would undoubtedly have impacted her thoughts on power-hungry men. The question of her marriage never went away in those early years, so Elizabeth surrounded herself with trusted ministers; her most loyal advisor was William Cecil, who she later created Lord Burghley; his son Robert would also go on to serve Elizabeth and her successor. The irony is that Elizabeth needed to surround herself with men – she had no choice in that, but the important fact remained that she was their queen and they were only her advisors; beyond that, they had no power over her person.

The Elizabethan era was a golden time for England, throughout her reign voyages of discovery set sail across the globe to unknown worlds to bring back exotic new spices, precious gems and the like. Sir Francis Drake and Sir Walter Raleigh both sailed to the Americas on expeditions in Elizabeth's name, which resulted in opening up new trading routes. In 1599, Elizabeth established the East India Company which again opened up a whole new world beyond the shores of England and Europe.

As trade boomed and England thrived, the arts also blossomed. Writers such as William Shakespeare, Ben Jonson and Christopher Marlowe were penning plays that were to be performed in the new open-air theatres like The Globe in Southwark on the south bank of the Thames. Elizabeth was said to be a fan of Shakespeare's plays but there is no evidence to suggest they were known to each other. Elizabethan manor houses, such as Hardwick Hall in Derbyshire and Burghley House in Lincolnshire, were being built by wealthy landowners and courtiers. The rooms were filled with fine furniture, while fine tapestries and glorious pieces of art adorned the walls. Despite the wealthy elite building new houses, Elizabeth herself did not commission any new palaces during her reign, unlike her father, who had been prolific in his commissioning of new buildings.

Like her father, and even more so as a woman, Elizabeth knew the importance of projecting the image of majesty. She wore glorious gowns with plunging necklines that were made from the finest of fabrics, the most sumptuous of jewels that sparkled like the sun and would certainly have dazzled her court under the candlelight of the 1500s. As queen, she had an army of ladies who would come to her in the morning to dress her ready for the day; as queen, she had to look flawless and that was a task that took up to two hours every day. She was presented with a new pair of shoes each week from her shoemaker, Garrett Johnston, whether she needed them or not! Elizabeth looked every inch a queen but was determined to rule like a king. As monarch, she liked to be seen by her people and would often take trips outside London so she could show herself to her subjects leaving them in no doubt as to who was ruling. These trips were called progresses and often took place in the summer. Not only were they a chance for Elizabeth to get out of London and meet her people, but they were also an opportunity for the London palaces to be aired and cleaned. Elizabeth was very good with the public, always knowing the right thing to say, and no doubt the poorer folk were delighted to meet their glorious queen. Despite her many travels, Elizabeth never ventured to the northern parts of her kingdom, preferring to stay in the south. Why this is we are not sure but the north was known as a Catholic hotbed with many rebellions having been formed there.

But for all her majesty, Elizabeth did not always sit easily on her throne. She was forever paranoid and convinced there were constant plots to steal the crown from her. The threats came from across Europe and in 1588, when Spain threatened to invade and conquer England, Elizabeth's navy won a historic victory over the Spanish Armada, no doubt spurred on by her stirring speech at Tilbury on 9 August:

> My loving people,
> We have been persuaded by some that are careful of our safety to take heed how we commit ourselves to armed multitudcs, for fcar of treachery. But I assure you, I do not desire to live to distrust my faithful and loving people.

> Let tyrants fear. I have always so behaved myself that, under God, I have placed my chiefest strength and safeguard in the loyal hearts and good-will of my subjects; and therefore I am come among you, as you see, at this time, not for my recreation and disport, but being resolved, in the midst and heat of the battle, to live and die among you all; to lay down for my God, and for my kingdom, and my people, my honour and my blood, even in the dust.
>
> I know I have the body of a weak and feeble woman; but I have the heart and stomach of a king, and of a king of England too, and think foul scorn that Parma or Spain, or any prince of Europe, should dare to invade the borders of my realm: to which rather than any dishonour shall grow by me, I myself will take up arms, I myself will be your general, judge, and rewarder of every one of your virtues in the field.
>
> I know already, for your forwardness you have deserved rewards and crowns; and We do assure you on a word of a prince, they shall be duly paid. In the mean time, my lieutenant general shall be in my stead, than whom never prince commanded a more noble or worthy subject; not doubting but by your obedience to my general, by your concord in the camp, and your valour in the field, we shall shortly have a famous victory over these enemies of my God, of my kingdom, and of my people.

The Spanish had intended to overthrow Elizabeth and Protestantism and replace her with Philip, or his daughter Isabella, whose claim we shall discuss in more detail later, and Catholicism. Philip believed he had a claim to the throne via his marriage to Queen Mary and a distant link to John of Gaunt, giving him – some would argue – a stronger claim than the Tudors.

Probably the biggest cause of anxiety for Elizabeth was the constant reminder that her cousin, Mary, Queen of Scots, was just one step from the English throne. The Scottish queen had fled her own country after she was forced to abdicate her crown in favour of her infant son James. She had been embroiled in a scandal that had seen her husband, Lord Darnley, murdered. Her subsequent marriage to the Earl of Bothwell, the chief suspect in Darnley's murder, did not help her cause. Ultimately, Mary had no choice but to throw herself on Elizabeth's mercy, but she was too much of a focus for rebellion to be allowed her freedom. On the insistence of Cecil, Elizabeth was urged not to help Mary regain her Scottish throne, but neither could she allow Mary to roam the Catholic courts of Europe, as it would have given her ample opportunity to raise an army to invade both England and Scotland. Elizabeth kept her rival under house arrest for nineteen years before finally executing her following Mary's supposed involvement in the Babington Plot, a plan that would have seen Elizabeth ousted from her throne.

Elizabeth would go on to reign for forty-five years and it is generally thought to be one of the most glorious and prosperous times in the country's history. Gloriana is the name attached to Queen Elizabeth I and her reign, a selfless woman who married her nation, who steered it through threats of war and booming trade. She created a constitutional crisis by refusing to marry and provide an heir, which led to decades of gossip, plotting and civil uncertainty. For someone who was forever paranoid, Elizabeth created a lot of the drama herself, but whoever was to succeed this queen would have huge shoes to fill.

Chapter Two

The Suffolk/Grey Claim

When Queen Elizabeth I ascended the throne of England in 1558, it was not clear at that stage who would succeed her, but at the age of 25, at the dawn of her reign, there would be time for those discussions to be had. There were certainly options available but each had its flaws, whether that be religion, politics or gender, but as the sun rose on the Elizabethan age, there were reasons to be optimistic, as the crown was lowered onto her flame-red Tudor hair, her new councillors would have expected the succession to be a distant concern.

Undoubtedly, Elizabeth was a paranoid person who was in constant fear that her throne could be taken from her by force at any moment, and if she gave birth to a son then her own child could become the focus of plots to oust her as queen. Maybe Elizabeth simply did not want to marry and have children, not all women do. We must also consider that childbirth at this time was perilous for both the mother and child, and there was a realistic chance that both could die during labour. Queens were not exempt from this; Elizabeth's own grandmother, Elizabeth of York, died while she was giving birth to her daughter in the Tower of London, which left her husband, Henry VII, and her children devastated.

So, had Elizabeth died while giving birth, the country would have been plunged into disaster; who would succeed her – especially if her child had died with her? Alternatively, what if Elizabeth died but the baby survived, and what if that child had been a girl rather than the much more desirable boy? Would Elizabeth's husband try to claim the crown for himself and rule in place of his child? Leaving an infant monarch could only bring trouble to a realm, James V of Scotland died when his daughter Mary was just 6 days old, so during her infancy regents had to be appointed to govern in her name. Firstly, Mary's heir James Hamilton, Earl of Arran, took the reins of power before Mary's mother, Marie de Guise, took over. Both regents had their enemies and opposition, leading to unrest and instability, Scotland remained teetering on a knife edge for years following Mary's birth; England would have wanted to avoid this scenario at all costs.

Given these potential outcomes, was Elizabeth right to remain unmarried? Yes, it was her duty, but wasn't it also her duty to keep her kingdom and people safe? She could have been bringing untold strife to the country by marrying; perhaps we will never know the exact reasons behind the queen's choice but she was certainly brave in making this decision. On a human level I think we must try to understand her reluctance to hand herself and her kingdom over to a husband who had no blood right to it. In her determination, she managed to keep her kingdom and her people safe by anticipating the trouble an unpopular marriage could cause. Regardless of the reasons behind Elizabeth's choice, the council had to look elsewhere for an heir to the throne of England.

One of the major sticking points when looking at the potential heirs to the Tudor throne was the last will of Henry VIII. As already noted above in The Last Will and Testament of King Henry VIII – An Author's Note, is a controversial document that affected both English and Scottish politics for much of the sixteenth century. At the time of Henry's death, the throne passed to his young son Prince Edward, no doubt Henry envisaged a long and happy reign for his son, one that would have provided him with plenty of heirs, so there would be no need to rely on extended family. Sadly, as we know, that plan did not work out; Edward died aged just 15 and Mary died childless.

The will of Henry VIII stated that if Elizabeth died childless then the children of Henry's younger sister Mary, Duchess of Suffolk and one time queen of France, would become the heirs. Princess Mary had married Charles Brandon, Duke of Suffolk, in a clandestine marriage in France in 1515 – against the wishes of the king. When he heard that his closest friend had defied his orders and married his beloved younger sister, the newlyweds were banished from court and were heavily fined. Henry forgave them soon enough and the marriage proved to be a fruitful and happy one. The Suffolks set up home at Westhorpe Hall in Suffolk and it was there they raised their children. They had two sons and two daughters, although sadly only Frances and Eleanor reached adulthood. The elder daughter, Frances, was born on 16 July 1517 at Hatfield in Hertfordshire, while her younger sister Eleanor followed just two years later, when she was born at Westhorpe. The sisters had a happy childhood in their mother's care and were later joined by their cousins Princess Mary and Margaret Douglas, the daughter of the elder Tudor sister, Margaret.

Margaret had been queen of Scotland and was the mother of James V, but when her husband James IV died, she remarried without the consent of the council. Her new husband, Archibald Douglas, Earl of Angus, had hoped to gain power through his wife but when she was punished for marrying without consent, he decided not to stick around and the marriage failed. He did, however, take care of his daughter and when things became heated in Scotland, he decided to send her to the English court where she was to be brought up by her uncle, Henry VIII. There was not really a place for Margaret in Scotland, despite being half-sister to the king; Angus felt she would prosper more south of the border, and it would turn out to be a good move for Margaret.

Both Frances and Eleanor knew from a young age that they were important and that their destiny in life was to marry well and have children. They would have been schooled by their mother in how to run a large household and estate and would be expected to marry well, for they were nieces to the king. For Frances the groom of choice was Henry Grey, Marquess of Dorset. He was of a similar age to his bride, and when he came of age at 21, he would be one of the richest men in the country bringing land, property and a title to Frances. The young couple were married at the age of 16 in 1533 at Suffolk Place, London, the home of her father, the duke. From the start they seemed like a good match for each other and got on well; in many arranged marriages, the feelings of the young couple were rarely taken into consideration and often they were unhappy unions. For Eleanor, the groom chosen by her father was Henry Clifford, the son and heir of Henry Clifford, 1st Earl of Cumberland. He was described as being tall and slim with flowing dark hair. They both worked in the household of Henry Fitzroy, Duke of Richmond and Somerset, the illegitimate son of Henry VIII, at Pontefract Castle in Yorkshire. Henry Clifford was created a Knight of the Bath at the coronation of Anne Boleyn. Their nuptials took place in June 1535 at the Church of St Mary Overies in London. In attendance was her uncle, the king, and we can only assume he was a guest at Frances's wedding too given they were said to enjoy a close relationship with their uncle.

In 1536/7 Frances gave birth to her first child, a daughter whom they named Jane, after Queen Jane Seymour. Lady Jane Grey was a young girl destined to be queen, even if it was for only nine days. Lady Jane became a pawn in the games of powerful men. Her parents were convinced to hand her over to Thomas Seymour, uncle of Edward VI and brother to the Lord Protector, on the promise that he would arrange her marriage to the young king, he also paid them a handsome fee. At the age of around 10 she packed her bags and moved to the household of Seymour and his new wife, the former queen and Henry VIII's widow, Katherine Parr. Thomas was a jealous but ambitious man who, as uncle to the king, felt he deserved a large slice of power. He resented the fact that his elder brother Edward, as Lord Protector, wielded so much authority and held so much influence with their young nephew.

His ambitions saw him face charges of treason and he was executed in March 1549, at which point Jane returned to her parents' care. Unfortunately, their care did not last long before she was married off to Guildford Dudley, the younger son of the all-powerful

John Dudley, Duke of Northumberland. Guildford was of a similar age to Jane and was just as much a pawn as she was in Northumberland's ruthless power grab. The duke's plan was to convince Edward VI, who was dying of suspected consumption, to name Jane as his heir and thereby putting his daughter-in-law on the throne as queen, alongside his son as king. Northumberland succeeded in amending the order of succession by convincing Edward to go against the wishes of his father by bypassing his half-sisters Mary and Elizabeth, as well as Frances and Eleanor. When Edward VI died in July 1553, at the age of 15, Lady Jane Grey took the throne as England's queen; her reign lasted just nine days and she was later executed on the orders of Queen Mary for assuming a crown that was not hers. Guildford, Northumberland, and Jane's father also lost their heads. With the eldest Grey sister dead before Elizabeth's reign even began, the next in line was the vivacious Lady Katherine Grey, and when Queen Mary died she became the focus of the Suffolk claim to the throne and with a younger sister following her, they looked in a strong position.

Lady Katherine Grey

Like her ill-fated elder sister, Katherine Grey's story is one of tragedy and heartbreak, but as Elizabeth ascended the throne, Katherine Grey was the recognised heir according to the last will of Henry VIII. We must, therefore, take Katherine's claim seriously because, after the queen, she was considered by many to be the most important woman in the realm.

Born on 25 August 1540 at her parents' country seat at Bradgate, Leicestershire, Lady Katherine Grey was the second of three daughters born to Frances and Henry Grey. It is widely believed that the Grey sisters spent much of their childhood at Bradgate, away from court life; given Henry VIII's mistrust of their father, he held no position at court, and so the girls were able to enjoy the tranquil settings of

Bradgate and grow up in relative solitude. Katherine would have been taught from an early age that she carried the blood of the royal house of Tudor and would have been acutely aware, as would all her sisters, of their noble and royal lineage. Henry Grey was a devout Protestant and he brought his daughters up in the new reformist religion; Jane would become a religious fanatic but Katherine, while committed to her religion, would never reach those same depths of zealousness that her elder sister and father did. The religious devotion led Henry to choose Protestant sympathisers for his daughters' tutors. The girls were well educated by the standards of the day and were taught Latin and Greek – Jane even went on to learn Hebrew.

It is well known that Jane was intellectually superior to both of her sisters, which has led many historians over the years to cast Katherine as the pretty, frivolous sister, and this label has caused her reputation to suffer. The problem that Katherine, and Mary too, faced was that they were forever compared to Jane, but the fact they were not as intelligent as their elder sister does not mean they were inferior in any way. All three sisters fell prey to men, but the difference was that both Katherine and Mary were the architects of their own downfall, whereas Jane was like a lamb to the slaughter. Although Katherine is often described as the prettiest of the three girls and Jane the cleverest, poor Mary didn't shine in either area; her appearance was affected by a physical deformity which has been described as causing her to have a crooked-back. She was cruelly described by one ambassador as being the ugliest person at court.

Much hope and planning went into Jane's future; she was going to marry the king one minute and be queen regnant the next, but when she did marry the chosen groom was the fourth son of the Duke of Northumberland, Guildford Dudley. Not much is known about Katherine's childhood other than it was spent predominantly in the Leicestershire countryside, but when her father became Duke of Suffolk in October 1551 the family's status rose even further and more time was spent in London and at court. Edward was on the throne and it seemed there would be more opportunities for Henry

Grey to serve his monarch. It was inevitable that all three girls would marry well. On 25 May 1553, at the wedding ceremony of Jane and Guildford, Katherine was married to Henry Herbert, the son and heir of the powerful and influential Earl of Pembroke; she was 12 years old. Marriage to a future earl was a very attractive prospect for Katherine would one day be a countess and have vast estates and properties to call her own. Mary was betrothed to Lord Grey of Wilton at the same time her elder sisters married, but that ceremony would have to wait given that she was only 8 years old. None of the girls had any say over who they married, it was their father's decision – although he was a weak man and could be cajoled into any scheme if pushed hard enough, and it was clear Northumberland was doing the pushing. That said, the king gave his blessing to all three marriages and even provided sums of money to pay for the wedding attire. The weddings took place at Durham House, the London residence of the Duke of Northumberland; the duke's daughter Katherine was also married that day to Henry Hastings, the son and heir of the Earl of Huntingdon. Following the three wedding ceremonies, a day of festivities were held, after which Katherine Grey went to live with her new husband's family at their impressive Thames-side home, Baynard's Castle. Unfortunately, the trail goes cold over Katherine's movements as events involving her sister Jane took over and began to spiral wildly out of control.

The events of July 1553 had a major impact on Katherine's life. Not only was she sister to the queen following the death of Edward VI, but when that reign came crashing down after just nine days, so did Katherine's marriage. When news reached London from East Anglia that Northumberland had failed in his quest to keep Jane on the throne, and that she had been deposed in favour of Mary Tudor, the Earl of Pembroke worked fast to sever all ties with the Grey family and sought an immediate annulment of Katherine and Henry's marriage. But the young couple were desperate to stay together, they had formed a loving and close relationship and told the earl that they had consummated their union, meaning it could not be annulled. It was a brave try, but given their young ages it is highly unlikely to be true; it was acceptable to marry at that age but it was certainly not acceptable to consummate a marriage at the age of 12.

It has been suggested that Katherine and her husband were at the Tower of London with Pembroke when Jane first arrived as queen on 10 July and stayed in residence until 19 July, when they likely moved back to Baynard's Castle. Katherine was her sister's heir and would become queen should Jane die without issue, but sadly we have no records detailing Katherine's thoughts or feelings regarding her sister's queenship and downfall. Although like everyone else, she was probably surprised and slightly bewildered to see her sister on the throne of England; did Katherine know much about what led to that moment, or had she been kept in the dark until the last minute? Despite being involved in events at the Tower, it is impossible to gauge if Katherine truly understood the danger her family was in. Once her marriage was annulled, she was to feel true heartbreak for the first time.

Katherine was said to be devastated when her marriage ended, she may have been young but she and Henry had bonded in the short time they had spent together. Through no fault of her own, she had to deal with the shame not only of having a sister who had usurped the throne, but also the embarrassment of being sent away from Baynard's Castle to return home to her parents at Charterhouse, Sheen. Katherine's melancholic state would certainly indicate her distress at being parted from Henry and it would be to him she turned in the future when in the midst of a scandal of her own making.

It is difficult to understand how much Katherine was told about her sister's fate, but when her father was initially pardoned and allowed home she could have been forgiven for thinking Jane would follow close behind. Sadly, her father took part in the Wyatt rebellion of 1554. This was a three-pronged attack led by Sir Thomas Wyatt of Kent in opposition to Queen Mary's proposed marriage the Prince Philip of Spain. The aim of the rebellion was to remove Queen Mary and replace her with Elizabeth and return the country to Protestantism.

The coordinated attacks were to come from the south-west, the Midlands and Kent. Suffolk led a failed attempt from Leicester and quickly retreated to his lands when it was clear the plan had failed. He was later found hiding in the hollow of a tree, he returned to London as a traitor and had assured a death warrant for both him and his eldest daughter; both were executed in February 1554. As Jane bravely faced her fate, Katherine was not far from her thoughts. Jane wrote to Katherine in her Greek New Testament:

> I Haue here sente you (good sister Katherin) a booke, which although it bee not outwardlye trimmed with golde, yet inwardly it is more worth then precious stones: it is the boke (dere Sister) of the lawe of the Lorde. It is his testament and last wil, which he bequethed vnto vs wretches, which shall lead you to the pathe of eternall ioye: and if you with a good mind read it, and with an earnest minde do folow it, it shal bring you to an immortall and euerlasting life. It wil teache you to liue, and learne you to die. It shal winne you more then you shoulde haue gained by the possession of your wofull fathers lāds. for, as if god had prospered him you shuld haue inherited his lāds: so if you apply diligētly this boke, sekyng to directe your life after it, you shalbe an inheritor of such riches, as nether the couetous shal withdraw from you, neither thefe shal steale, nether yet the mothes corrupt. Desyre with Dauid (good sister) tunderstād the law of the lord your god: liue stil to die, that you (by death) may purchase eternal lyfe. And truste not that the tenderousnes of your age shal lēghthen your life. For as soone (if God call) goeth the yong as the olde: & labour alwayes to learn to die, de e the worlde, denye the deuill, and despise the eshe, and delite your selfe onely in the Lord. Be penitent for your sinnes, and yet despaire not: be strong in faith, & yet presume not, and desire with

> saint Paule to be dissolued, and to be with Christ, with whom euē in death ther is life. Be like the good seruaunt, & euen at mid night be waking, lest when death commeth and stealeth vpon you like a thefe in the nighte, you be with the euyll seruaunt found sleping, & lefte for lacke of oyle, you be founde like the ue foolish women, and lyke hym that had not on the weddyng garment, and then ye be cast out from the mariage. Reioyce in Christ, as I trust I do. Folow the steppes of your maister Christ, and take vp your crosse, lay your sinnes on his back and alwaies embrace him. And as touching my death, reioyce as I doe (good Sister) that I shal be deliuered of this corruption, and put on incorruption. For I am assured that I shall for losyng of a mortall lyfe, wynne an immortal lyfe, the whiche I praye God graunt you, sende you of his grace to liue in his feare, and to die in the true christian fayth, from the whiche (in Gods name) I exhort you that you neuer swarue, neither for hope of life, nor for feare of death. For if ye wyl deny his truth to lenghthen youre lyfe, God wyll denye you, and yet shorten youre dayes. And if you will cleaue vnto him, he will prolong your dayes to your comforte and hys glory, to the whiche glory god bring me nowe, and you hereafter when it pleaseth hym to call you. Fare you well (good Sister) and put your onely trust in god, who onely muste helpe you.

The letter was taken from *Acts and Monuments Volume VI* by John Foxe, and if we assume this letter is authentic, we have no record of Katherine's reaction to receiving it. There is also no record of Jane having written to her mother or Mary. Katherine was just 13 when her sister and father were executed; she had one failed marriage behind her and with no father or elder sister to guide her the future looked very uncertain. The Grey family had been decimated and it looked as though they had lost royal favour for good. The actions of Henry

Grey, Duke of Suffolk, appeared to have ruined the chances of any of his daughters being able to claim the English throne (I do not ascribe any fault to Jane; she was cajoled and bullied into taking a throne she knew was not hers to take). It was to be hoped that Katherine and Mary had learnt a valuable lesson that the wrath of a monarch often meant death, regardless of family loyalty and status – and definitely regardless of royal standing. It was a brutal time in which to live and the closer to the throne you stood, the more careful you had to be.

Frances, Katherine and Mary now had to forge a new path together at the court of Queen Mary I. Thankfully, Frances had always been close to her cousin and places were soon found for them. Frances was made a lady of the privy chamber and it is probable Katherine joined her; given Mary's young age it is likely she was not given an official role. It wasn't long before Katherine was being touted as Mary's heir, but that was no foregone conclusion because in July 1554, Mary married Philip II of Spain at Winchester Cathedral. Despite being 37 at the time of her marriage, Mary would have been expecting to have a son and heir to follow her.

Katherine's claim to the throne had always been questioned. There was speculation that her parents' marriage was invalid because before his marriage to Frances, Henry Grey had been precontracted to Katherine Fitzalan, daughter of the 11th Earl of Arundel. If this was true then the Grey sisters were illegitimate and could have no claim. Where this rumour started is not known. At the time of Henry and Frances's marriage her father had paid for the precontract to be ended, backed by Henry VIII himself. However, there would have been factions at court, mainly Catholic, that would not have wanted the Protestant Katherine to succeed and would have looked towards Margaret Douglas as an alternative.

Many felt Elizabeth was the rightful heir, despite an uneasy relationship between the two half-sisters; if Henry's will was to be adhered to, then his youngest daughter should follow her sister. There is mention of Katherine and Mary's place in the order of succession by the Imperial Ambassador Simon Renard, who wrote to his master, the emperor, to advise that the Grey sisters had not been tainted by the downfall of their sister and father. They may still have their places in the line of succession, but thanks to Henry Grey's charge of treason, the family estates had been confiscated and forfeited back to the Crown – although in April 1554, Mary returned the manors in Leicestershire back to Frances, which meant she had some income to support herself and her daughters. Frances also decided to remarry, which took many by surprise, as it was only months after her husband's execution. Her new husband was Adrian Stokes, her Master of the Horse; it was an interesting choice of groom but by marrying a man so far beneath her in status, Frances forfeited any claim she may have had on the Crown. Instead, she retired from court life to live peacefully with her new husband and Mary, while Katherine remained at court. Katherine more than likely enjoyed a friendly relationship with Queen Mary and it appeared she bore her no ill will over the executions of Jane and her father, and likewise Mary did not hold the fact that she was a Grey against Katherine.

As Queen Mary knew, in order for her to stay secure on her throne it was going to be vital for her to marry and produce an heir, but her choice of marriage to Philip of Spain was not popular among her advisors. Their biggest concern was that England would be consumed by the all-powerful Spain and become nothing but a satellite state. But Mary did not heed the warnings and was adamant she was going to marry into her beloved Spanish family (the emperor Charles V was her cousin and Philip's father, and both were descended from John of Gaunt). She ensured her wedding ceremony at Winchester Cathedral was a grand affair as befitted a ruling queen. Winchester was a significant choice of venue as it was the birthplace of her uncle, Prince Arthur, in 1486; and held a sense of righteousness and reinforced the Tudors' right to rule through their Welsh connection to King Arthur. Katherine was probably in attendance at the wedding, but sadly we have no proof of this.

On 31 March 1555, Katherine stood as godmother to Elizabeth Cavendish. Elizabeth was the daughter of Sir William Cavendish and the influential Bess of Hardwick. Katherine was thriving and as she grew into her role at court she forged a close friendship with Lady Jane Seymour, daughter of the old Lord Protector, the executed Duke of Somerset, and niece of Queen Jane Seymour. The two young women were of similar ages and backgrounds, they could empathise with each other, given that they had both lost their fathers on the executioner's block. In the summer of 1555, the court was a joyous and happy place as the queen announced she was pregnant. Given her close proximity to Mary, it is likely Katherine was nearby as the events of that year unfolded, but we must bear in mind that she probably split her time equally between being at court and at home with her mother, whom she appears to have enjoyed a close relationship with. Frances's reputation as a cruel and abusive mother comes from an account written by Lady Elizabeth's tutor, Roger Ascham. He was a regular visitor to Bradgate and wrote that Jane suffered terribly at the hands of her parents. The account was only published in 1570, several years after those involved had died, meaning there is no contemporary evidence to support this claim. There was also never any indication that she acted in this manner towards Katherine or Mary.

Sadly, the happy atmosphere at court did not last long when it became clear to all that the queen was not pregnant and had suffered what many believe to be a 'phantom pregnancy'. The doctors agreed that all the signs indicated Mary was with child, and so, on their advice, she entered her confinement as normal. When no baby had arrived by the end of the summer the queen suffered great embarrassment and humiliation. When she left her birthing chamber Philip decided to make his way back to Europe, leaving Mary distraught and desolate at his abandonment of her. Naturally, the lack of a child prompted speculation over who Mary's successor would be – would Princess Elizabeth take the throne as many expected, or would Katherine Grey swoop in and steal it away from under the nose of another royal Tudor, just as her sister had?

The Imperial Ambassador Simon Renard wrote to his master the emperor claiming that Mary had considered having Elizabeth declared a bastard, which meant she would be unable to claim the throne. He also goes on to explain that had she been successful in getting this through Parliament, the door would be open for Mary's cousin Margaret Douglas, Countess of Lennox, to take the throne. Margaret was Mary's preferred choice given the close relationship they had shared since childhood and the fact that Margaret was a devout Catholic. If Mary were to name Margaret as her heir, that would mean defying her father's wishes because he had stipulated that the Scottish line of his elder sister Margaret was to be discounted from the line of succession. Margaret Douglas, who was half-sister to the Scottish king, James V, was Margaret's only daughter, and the fact that she had been born and raised in England would have bolstered her claim. As it turned out, the plan to illegitimise Elizabeth came to nothing, but did expressing her wish for Margaret to be her heir demonstrate Mary's intention to favour her over Katherine? Maybe the queen felt the treasonous acts of her family barred Katherine from the throne, but it was more likely to have been a religious decision more than anything. Katherine was fighting this battle on two fronts: one, because many felt she should be forced to forfeit her right to the throne due to the actions of Jane and her father; and two, many believed she was illegitimate due to her parents' marriage being invalid. But Katherine had her supporters, mainly from Protestants who wanted to see the return of their religion. As far as they were concerned, the last thing the country needed was a continuation of the Catholic faith. Also, in reality, the validity of the Suffolks' marriage had long been settled; it was nothing more than a weak excuse for people to turn against Katherine and her family.

In 1555, Katherine travelled to Hanworth, the family seat of her good friend Lady Jane Seymour. Jane was ill and was taking time away from her court duties to go home and convalesce. It was during this trip that Katherine met Jane's elder brother Edward Seymour, Earl of Hertford, for the first time. The two had an instant connection and Lady Jane quickly became the go-between for the couple and before long a relationship developed. Katherine had long maintained her love for her first husband Henry Herbert, but that summer there was a clear shift in her affections when she declared herself enamoured with Lord Hertford. Not everyone at Hanworth was pleased with the news. Hertford's mother, the redoubtable Anne Stanhope, dowager Duchess of Somerset strongly advised her son to stay away from Katherine, but he ignored her and instead asked his sister to approach the subject of marriage with Katherine. Sadly, there is no record that tells us how the relationship progressed at this stage and before long Katherine and Jane Seymour returned to court. Court was a sombre place to be as it was clear Queen Mary had been ill for some time and those around her knew she was dying.

In early November, she named her half-sister Elizabeth as her heir. Whether Katherine was ever a realistic option to take Mary's throne is unknown, but Mary chose to honour her father's will and pass the crown on to Elizabeth. Sadly, there is no record as to Katherine's feelings but in all honesty, she probably never harboured any real hopes that Mary would name her as successor and probably knew better than to risk taking the throne from the rightful heir. Queen Mary died on the morning of 17 November 1558 at St James's Palace; her husband Philip II stated he 'felt a reasonable regret for her death'. With her death came the dawn of a new wonderous age for England, but for Katherine Grey, it would be far from glorious.

Katherine could be forgiven for assuming her place within the privy chamber was assured, after all she shared the same royal blood as the new queen and was heir presumptive, if the will of Henry VIII was to be followed. Sadly, she was mistaken. Her relationship with Elizabeth was very different from the one she had shared with Mary.

Elizabeth was just 25 years old when she came to the throne and everyone, including Katherine, had no reason to think the queen would not marry and have children of her own. So, while Katherine may have entertained the notion that she might one day be queen, she waited to see who Elizabeth would marry; would she choose an English noble, or look to foreign shores as her sister had?

Elizabeth was crowned at Westminster Abbey on 15 January 1559, Katherine would have been present in the abbey but if she played a role in the actual ceremony, it has not been recorded. Elizabeth was a naturally paranoid person and was always looking over her shoulder for any potential usurpers. Katherine was a physical reminder to Elizabeth that while she remained unmarried and childless – and whether she liked it or not – Katherine was her heir. As with any political decision in Tudor England, religion played a part. Katherine was a committed Protestant, as was Elizabeth, which meant the other claimant to Elizabeth's throne – the Catholic Mary, Queen of Scots – was at a disadvantage. Mary had dismissed Elizabeth's role as queen and had herself publicly proclaimed the true queen of England; she even went as far as having the royal arms of Scotland, the arms of her husband, Francois, Dauphin of France, quartered with those of England. These arrogant actions enraged Elizabeth and strengthened the support for Katherine's claim.

Mary's claim was dynastically stronger than Katherine's, but the Scottish claim had previously been discounted and the English would undoubtedly have preferred an English monarch over a Scottish one – particularly one who had married into France. From our modern-day perspective it is difficult to comprehend just how strong Katherine's claim was at this time. We have the benefit of hindsight and the knowledge that James VI succeeded Elizabeth, but there were many names throughout Elizabeth's reign with a legitimate claim and Katherine's was the most prominent – she was referred to in Henry's will, and she was a Protestant.

So, as it stood in 1559, Elizabeth Tudor was the unmarried queen of England and Lady Katherine Grey was her heir presumptive. Given her prominent role in the line of succession more records were starting to be kept of Katherine's movements. She is described by the Imperial Ambassador, the Count of Feria, as being a friend of his, and he was someone whom she confided. Katherine told the count she believed Elizabeth did not want her to succeed and that she felt slighted at being made a Lady of the Bedchamber rather than of the Privy Chamber. She went on to confirm to Feria that she would remain a Catholic (during the reign of Mary I, it was advised to portray yourself as a Catholic even if you were not) and not convert back to Protestantism. Spain would not have wanted the French-backed Mary, Queen of Scots, to take the English throne, so this was music to Feria's ears; it meant Catholic Spain could control Katherine and arrange a marriage for her that would suit their own needs, believing that one day they would control England through its Catholic queen.

There have been suggestions that the sudden elevation in Katherine's status went to her head and she was often heard speaking in an arrogant and boastful manner, which the queen herself overheard. This would have done nothing to help repair their relationship, which appears to have been fractured from the moment Elizabeth became queen. It is no secret that she did not like Katherine but the reasons for her displeasure are not fully understood.

The pressure Elizabeth faced to marry and produce the all-important Tudor heir was immense. As time went, on her council tried their best to persuade the queen to take a husband, they badgered her constantly; as far as they were concerned, it was her duty to the country to ensure the succession was a smooth and peaceful transition. It begs the question: if they had not pushed her so hard, would she have relented? As it was, she dug her heels in and told her advisors that she was in no rush to marry. She saw marriage and having a child as God's will, and if it was destined to happen, then it would. There were plenty of suitors lining up to make her an offer. At the head of the list were the Dukes of Ferrara, Savoy and Saxony, and there was even talk of the King of Sweden offering his hand to the queen, but choosing any foreign groom would have to be done with great care. The council had learnt from the marriage of Mary and Philip of Spain, which proved to be a hugely unpopular choice – incidentally, Philip himself was considered a prospective suitor for Elizabeth at one time but she wisely declined the hand of her former brother-in-law.

If a foreign groom was not chosen then it would have to be an Englishman and that in itself brought a new set of issues. Elizabeth's favourite was Robert Dudley, but he was already married to Amy Robsart; when Amy died in 1560 in suspicious circumstances it ended all possibility of a union between the two as suspicion fell at Robert's door. However, Elizabeth remained close to Dudley and it has often been suggested that the two were in fact lovers and so marriage for Elizabeth would have ended that. As mentioned earlier, a particular issue with marrying within England is the risk of promoting a noble family to greater heights than others would have liked – with Elizabeth's maternal family being a case in point. The Boleyn family reached incredible heights when Anne married Henry VIII, but that did not end well, as we know. The Boleyn family were left in the wilderness until Elizabeth came to power when she was keen to promote and support members of her extended family. The council became exasperated with her reluctance to marry and finally told her to choose whomever she wanted; the most important thing was that she marry and have a legitimate heir to prolong the Tudor dynasty.

While the council and Elizabeth were bickering over her marriage, or lack of marriage, the Spanish were plotting to kidnap Katherine and marry her to Carlos, Prince of Asturias and eldest son of Philip II. As royalty, Katherine could only marry with the consent of the queen and it was highly unlikely Elizabeth would consent to a Spanish match. The rumour circulating at court was that the Ladies Montague and Hungerford, along with the Countess of Feria, were to lure Katherine aboard a ship which would set sail for Spain. There is no evidence that Katherine had any prior knowledge of the plot but unbeknownst to Carlos, Feria and Philip, her heart lay with someone else: the Earl of Hertford.

The relationship between Katherine and Hertford was heating up fast. They met in private with the help of Jane Seymour and before long he was proposing marriage again. Knowing Katherine's marriage was of significance, he approached her mother Frances in October 1559 to seek her approval. Frances discussed the proposal with her husband,

Adrian Stokes, and they both agreed Hertford was an appropriate husband for her daughter and they would be happy for them to wed – providing Elizabeth agreed to the match. Frances knew full well what it was like to lose royal favour and knew full well that Elizabeth needed to be consulted; she had lost one daughter to the executioner's axe she did not want to lose another. Stokes advised Hertford to approach those members of the council who favoured him to seek their approval. In the meantime, Frances agreed to write to Elizabeth directly to seek her favour and ask for Katherine to be excused from court to visit her mother at Charterhouse. Elizabeth agreed and when Katherine arrived, Frances told her daughter of Hertford's visit and request, we can only imagine how excited Katherine would have been as she told her mother she was willing to marry him. Satisfied that her daughter was happy with the proposal Frances agreed to write to Elizabeth asking for consent to the marriage. Sadly, that letter was never written as Frances fell ill and died on 20 November 1559, aged 42. The death of Frances came as a huge blow to the couple's plans, not only was Katherine grieving for her mother but she had to do it without the man she loved at her side. Frances was buried on 5 December at Westminster Abbey; despite her disdain towards Frances, Elizabeth gave her cousin a lavish funeral and Katherine performed the role of chief mourner, with Mary following behind.

While Katherine and Hertford's relationship was blossoming the Spanish interest did not abate and news soon reached Elizabeth that Katherine was the focus of a Spanish plot. The queen's response was to return Katherine to royal favour – she even went as far as calling Katherine her daughter. She gave her sumptuous rooms and began to make a fuss of her, but this was all for show as everyone knew there was no love lost between the two cousins. Elizabeth was being clever; she knew that by favouring Katherine this way, she was making it clear that Mary, Queen of Scots, was not alone in her claim to the throne. Aware that the Spanish were trying to get their hands on Katherine, showing favour to her in such a luxurious and open way was a clear signal that Katherine was hers, not Spain's.

The Scots were also getting in on the act by suggesting Katherine marry James Hamilton, 3rd Earl of Arran and descendant of James II. Arran was in the line of succession for the Scottish throne, and the Scots harboured hopes of uniting the thrones of Scotland and England. In this, they underestimated their current queen, Mary. Elizabeth would not have consented to the marriage – or any marriage that involved Katherine in fact, partly because she did not like her, and partly because the idea of Katherine producing a male heir would have worried the queen greatly.

Katherine and Hertford married at some point between November and December 1560, without prior agreement from Elizabeth. The marriage would bring Elizabeth's wrath down so hard that Katherine would never recover. Does the fact that Katherine married without consent show that she did not see herself as Elizabeth's heir? She would have known she needed permission to marry, and what the punishment could be when she was found out. Clearly she had not learnt from her sister's fate, or maybe she was so blinded by love that she had no care for the consequences. She either must have believed she could talk Elizabeth round, or that her love for Hertford was greater than any love she bore for the Crown. But what of Hertford? Were his plans for marrying Katherine honourable and true? Did he risk everything, potentially his life, for his undying love for Katherine? Or did he perhaps have bigger ambitions to be king and used Katherine as the vehicle to grasp power? His father, the Lord Protector, and his Uncle Thomas were both power-grabbing men, and they both ended their lives at the executioner's block. It was all very reminiscent of Katherine's sister Jane and her tragic downfall at the hands of ambitious men – except Katherine was more in control of the situation; she went into her marriage with her eyes wide open and fully aware of the consequences. Perhaps Hertford too had been blinded by love; but he knew full well how dangerous it was to upset a Tudor monarch.

With the help of Lady Jane Seymour, it was agreed that the couple would marry as soon as the queen was away from the palace, which would mean Katherine could slip away unseen to make her way to Hertford's home on Canon Row, London. On the day, of which neither Katherine nor Hertford could confirm when they were later questioned, the earl dismissed his servants while Katherine pleaded illness in order to be excused from her duties. An hour after the queen had left the palace, Katherine and Jane made their way in secret to Hertford, who had arranged for the wedding bands to be made at a goldsmith in Fleet Street. When the two ladies arrived, Jane left to find a priest who would be willing to perform the ceremony. A priest was found and performed the wedding ceremony that united Lady Katherine Grey and Edward Seymour, Earl of Hertford. In their joy neither of the newlyweds thought to take the name of the priest, or his parish, something they would later live to regret. Following the ceremony the couple consummated their union after which Katherine and Jane returned to court with no one suspecting a thing.

Once married, the newlyweds met in secret on a regular basis with the help of Jane; sadly, she died just a few months later, leaving the couple without a go-between – and even more crucially, without a witness to their nuptials. But the death of Jane was not the only crisis Katherine had to deal with as she began to believe she was pregnant. When she divulged these fears to Hertford, he admitted there was nothing they could do except hope the queen would be merciful when she eventually found out the truth. It must have been a terrifying time.

Katherine did not just lose a friend and Hertford a sister when Jane died, but also the one person, other than the priest, who witnessed their wedding ceremony. She was the only person who could testify that the nuptials had happened and before long the lack of witnesses was going to prove a disaster for them. Rather remarkably, Hertford applied for permission to travel to Europe but before he left, he made Katherine a gift of £1,000 a year for her to live on. Sadly she could not recount the day her husband gave her the relevant paperwork, or where she had put it. It seems a strange thing for Hertford to do, after all he was a newlywed and about to become a father – although Katherine could not say for certain that she was pregnant. In those days the only certain way of knowing you were with child was when the woman felt the baby 'quicken' in her womb. Hertford was adamant he would not leave her if she could guarantee she was pregnant. His behaviour around this time does seem rather strange given his situation, had he got cold feet and was worried about what the retaliation would be to the news of his and Katherine's marriage? He comes across as being rather unmanly, surely he should have stayed by his wife's side and taken the punishment together.

Hertford made his way to France where he attended the coronation of Charles IX at Rheims. While he was away Cecil took the opportunity to advise Katherine to be aware of any attention Hertford may give her – clearly the couple had not been as discreet as they thought. If Cecil had concerns, then it must have been obvious to some that the couple were closer than they ought to have been. Unfortunately, she did not take the opportunity to confide her current situation to Cecil. If she had, then things may have turned out for the better; instead, she kept quiet. Cecil supported Katherine's claim to the throne and he worked hard to promote her – the last thing he needed was an ill-judged marriage, hence his warning to her. Her marriage would be of dynastical importance and not one she should be frivolous with. When news of the marriage broke throughout the court, Cecil must have felt a huge wave of disappointment and anger. It would also have been his job to try and soothe the queen's anger.

Katherine heard no news from Hertford while he was away except for a delivery of a pair of bracelets, but he sent gifts to other people too, so he was certainly not marking his wife out for any special attention. She had no replies to her letters, had Katherine's friends been right all along? Was Hertford bad news? Life was extremely complicated for Katherine and before long another problem raised its head. The father of her first husband, Henry Herbert, made the bold suggestion that they should remarry; clearly the Earl of Pembroke had seen the error of his ways all those years before when he had rashly annulled the marriage of his son and heir to Katherine Grey, despite the young husband and wife begging to be allowed to stay together. Over time Katherine's feelings towards Herbert had cooled, but that did not mean he could not be of use to her now.

With Hertford's continued silence Katherine knew she would need a protector over the coming months. For all she knew, Hertford could deny their marriage had ever happened and in turn deny he was the father of her unborn child, leaving her reputation in tatters. The anxiety she must have felt over the days and weeks following Hertford's absence must have been almost unbearable. Katherine knew only too well how angry the queen could get; how would she react when she discovered that her potential heir had married without her permission and then fallen pregnant? The summer came and with Hertford still away on the Continent, Katherine accompanied the queen on her summer progress. Also part of the retinue was Henry Herbert, with the hope of remarrying Katherine, he spent much of his time with her – but all that would change when he discovered her pregnancy. He called her a whore and reminded her that they had been legally divorced many years ago; he was determined she would not bring him down to her gutter level. Along with the insults, he also asked her to return any letters and tokens he had sent to her and with that the Herberts washed their hands of Katherine Grey for a second time.

Worse still was the threat he made to expose Katherine's secrets to the court – which meant time was fast running out. She could keep her secret no longer, it was time to face up to her situation – and the queen. People were now openly gossiping about Katherine and her current state, her pregnancy had begun to show and her gown would not have allowed much wiggle room to conceal her swollen belly. She knew people were talking about her and in the first instance she turned to a lady called Elizabeth Stenlow, a member of the queen's privy chamber. Katherine looked to her for guidance, but sadly Stenlow was unable to provide the comfort and reassurance she had been looking for. She also turned to Bess of Hardwick, knowing she was close to the queen and might be able to smooth the road for her. She too declined to get involved.

In a last-ditch attempt for help, she turned to her one-time kinsman and the queen's favourite, Robert Dudley. She decided to approach him while the court was staying at Ipswich and here she divulged every last detail to him, pleading with him to intercede on her behalf with Elizabeth. He agreed to do what he could, but even he could not placate the queen's anger when she heard to news. Apoplectic with rage, Elizabeth ordered Katherine's arrest and insisted she be sent straight to the Tower to be held as a prisoner. The queen also wrote to France demanding that Hertford return home immediately to answer questions regarding his behaviour. Katherine may have been a prisoner at the Tower but do not be fooled into thinking she was kept in a cold dark dungeon like so many of its other notorious residents. Katherine had royal blood, so she was kept in a suite of rooms that were well furnished with furniture from the royal stores that had previously belonged to Henry VIII. She had a luxurious bed to sleep in, a chair covered in cloth of gold and a rich purple velvet cushion. I wonder if her thoughts ever strayed to her elder sister Jane, who had been incarcerated and executed just seven years earlier; could she be about to face the same fate? If she did, what would become of her unborn child?

On 17 August 1561 Queen Elizabeth ordered Sir Edward Warner, the Lieutenant of the Tower, to interrogate Katherine over her marriage to Hertford but she could tell him very little. Elizabeth Stenlow was also sent to the Tower for her failure to immediately disclose to the queen what she knew. In France, Hertford had received the queen's summons which had been written in a manner that suggested he and Katherine would be treated well and that he was required just to determine the legality of the marriage. Of course, this was just a ruse; when he stepped back on English soil, he was promptly arrested and sent to join his wife in the Tower, albeit in separate quarters.

Katherine and Hertford were now both prisoners of Elizabeth and all they could do was wait and hope that she would be lenient with them. The news of their marriage and subsequent arrest spread fast but the validity of the nuptials was called into question as neither of them could give a matching account and there were no witnesses available to verify the ceremony had actually taken place. They were asked many questions about the ceremony, and about the priest and Jane's involvement; they even went as far as being asked which side of the bed each had lain on. Many servants were called for questioning, as was Katherine's stepfather Adrian Stokes, and Hertford's brother, Henry. Despite the interrogation and Katherine's production of the wedding band, the judgement was that the marriage was invalid and any child born of it would be deemed illegitimate. All of this now meant she would be seen as an unsuitable candidate to inherit the throne. Naturally, the blame for this all fell on Katherine; as the woman, she must have lured Hertford into her bed and overpowered him with her female charms. She was seen as a whore – and a pregnant one at that, but to Hertford's credit he stood by his wife.

Katherine's spectacular fall from grace spurred on the supporters of Mary, Queen of Scots, but she soon regained the upper hand when, on 21 September 1561, she gave birth to a healthy baby boy – Edward Seymour, who assumed the title of Lord Beauchamp. A healthy Protestant boy with royal blood in his veins was surely going to be seen as an ideal candidate to succeed Elizabeth; he may have been deemed illegitimate, but that could be dealt with. After all, Henry VIII had declared Mary and Elizabeth illegitimate but still named them in the order of succession, and both had ruled as queen.

As per the Treason Act of 1536, it was deemed an offence punishable by death to marry a member of the royal family without the monarch's permission, and so Elizabeth was well within her rights to have Katherine and Hertford arrested and executed. Katherine's behaviour was seen as a reflection on Elizabeth; her ladies were the embodiment of the queen and she had to be seen to have full authority and control over her household. The marriage saga raised the subject of the succession yet again, Elizabeth was now ready to discount Katherine and Mary Grey completely, given their father and sisters' treason, so at this time, Mary, Queen of Scots, was probably her preferred choice. The problem was that Elizabeth was constantly paranoid that there were plots to remove her from her throne and Katherine's marriage was seen by her as such a plot – although Cecil did not believe it was anything more than two reckless young lovers making unwise choices.

Lord Beauchamp was baptised at the Tower of London chapel of St Peter ad Vincula, not far from where the body of his Aunt Jane lay. The baby boy certainly strengthened his mother's claim to the throne – providing it could be proven that the wedding between his parents had taken place and was a legal and valid ceremony. If that could be done, then one day Edward Seymour could sit on the throne of England.

In February, Katherine and Hertford were interviewed by Matthew Parker, Archbishop of Canterbury, in the hope that he would be able to pass judgement one way or the other concerning the validity of their marriage. He did reach a verdict and it was officially decreed that the marriage was invalid and the children born of it illegitimate. There are no records to tell us how Katherine felt about the ruling but one can imagine her heartbreak. What we do know is that she continued to meet with her husband despite being held in different rooms at the Tower. Either Katherine or Hertford somehow managed to convince the Lieutenant to allow the earl to visit his wife in her rooms. The first clandestine meeting took place on 25 May and then again on the 29th. Each time the guards left them alone – following hefty bribes no doubt. On the third attempt Hertford found his wife's rooms locked against him, but the damage had already been done; Katherine was pregnant for a second time. Hertford was to stand trial in the Star Chamber for breaking prison rules and for bedding Katherine again, he was fined the enormous sum of £15,000 (approximately £3.5 million today). Thankfully, he was not expected to pay the sum in one go. The reckless behaviour of both Katherine and Herford is quite something to behold. They had been punished for their marriage and the subsequent birth of their first child, but to stupidly put themselves in that situation again is mind boggling – the threat of execution was clearly not enough to keep this pair separate.

As Queen Elizabeth continued to refuse to marry and also declined to name her successor, many councillors and courtiers continued to lend their support to Katherine. A portrait miniature of Katherine and her eldest son, Lord Beauchamp, was commissioned and painted by Flemish artist Levina Teerlinc in around 1561. It is interesting to note that this was painted after the marriage had been declared unlawful, yet she is stated as Countess of Hertford and proudly shows off her first-born son. She is also painted wearing her wedding band and a portrait of her husband around her neck. Katherine is being portrayed as a wife and mother. By painting mother and son together, the artist is potentially showing the next two monarchs of England.

The succession crisis was to become all too real when the queen fell ill with smallpox in 1562; not many people survived this terrible disease so it was a very worrying time. The battlelines were drawn. On one side there were the Protestants, headed up by Katherine and her son, and on the other side were the Catholics, whose main candidates were Mary, Queen of Scots and Margaret Douglas, Countess of Lennox – although she herself was a prisoner of Elizabeth's over her involvement the marriage between her son, Lord Darnley, and Mary, Queen of Scots.

If the wishes of Henry VIII were to be followed then Katherine was next in line and ought to wear the crown. Those who considered the will invalid backed the Scottish Catholic claim. In the end it was all irrelevant as the queen made a full recovery – but this had certainly been a wake-up call. The queen was not invincible and an air of anxiety and uncertainty lingered over the court.

With the tension mounting, a brave group of nobles, led by the Duke of Norfolk publicly declared their support for Katherine; when Elizabeth heard of this, she took immediate action by weakening Katherine's claim. Elizabeth now decided to switch her support to the potential claim of Henry Stuart, Lord Darnley. Darnley was the eldest son of Elizabeth's cousin Margaret Douglas and so had royal Tudor blood in his veins but, crucially, he was a Catholic. Did Elizabeth not consider religion to be a deciding factor when it came to nominating her heir? Or was she just merely playing games again? There will be more on his claim later, but while Elizabeth was championing the handsome young Darnley, Katherine gave birth to her second son at the Tower. We do not know the exact date Thomas Seymour was born, but it is thought he made his first appearance in late 1561/early 1562. Like his elder brother, he was baptised at St Peter ad Vincula within the Tower precincts. Thomas was a healthy baby boy who bolstered Katherine's claim even further, and it seemed the invalidity of her marriage was of no hindrance to her. She had shown she could produce healthy male children, and a healthy stock of sons in the royal nursery would have made her a very plausible candidate. The question was, would Katherine rule independently, or would her eldest son take the throne over her?

In reality the invalidity of her marriage and the illegitimacy of her sons is an irrelevant point, the fact she was a Protestant with royal blood in her veins made her claim valid, and if she did become queen then the first thing she would do is validate her marriage and legitimise her sons. Elizabeth's insistence that the invalidity of Katherine's marriage and the illegitimacy of her sons made her claim weak is a fragile argument.

The summer of 1563 brought the plague to London and that in turn forced Elizabeth to release the Hertfords from the Tower, but not from their imprisonment. Edward was sent to live with his mother at Hanworth taking Lord Beauchamp with him, while Katherine went with baby Thomas to live under house arrest with her uncle, Lord John Grey, at Pirgo in Essex. The split with her eldest son must have broken Katherine's heart even further. Little did she know that when she handed him over at the Tower it would be the last time she would ever see him or her husband. During their enforced separation Katherine and Hertford corresponded frequently and despite the distance between them their love never waned. The time Katherine spent with her uncle fluctuated and there were occasions when she thought Elizabeth would forgive her and restore her to royal favour which bolstered her mood, but other times she fell into a pit of despair; anguished and missing her husband.

If Katherine desired forgiveness she did not help her cause by signing her letters to the queen in her married name, Katherine Hertford – this did nothing but antagonise Elizabeth even further. She had little in the way of money which meant she was unable to buy new clothes for herself or Thomas. A request was made via Cecil and Dudley that Hertford send his wife a payment of £114 (approximately £25,000 today) to pay for the upkeep of his wife and child. Cecil, Dudley and John Grey all wrote to Elizabeth in the hope that she might relent and pardon the Hertfords, but it all fell on deaf ears and John Grey even found himself locked in the Tower for his troubles; sadly, he was to die in November 1564. Due to this incarceration, Katherine and Thomas were moved into the care of Sir William Petre of Ingatestone Hall; he had been a secretary of State for three Tudor monarchs and still remained an important part of Elizabeth's court. Hertford was also on the move; he was sent to reside with Sir John Mason while Lord Beauchamp stayed with his grandmother at Hanworth.

Katherine did not stay anywhere for long and soon enough she was being moved from Ingatestone to Gosfield Hall, the home of Sir John Wentworth and his family, where she stayed for over a year. Many people still petitioned Elizabeth to forgive Katherine, or at least show some leniency to her. The queen's treatment of her kinswoman was not popular and the dowager Duchess of Somerset even went to court to plead directly with Cecil and Dudley to help them. It would seem her secretary and favourite were powerless to do anything. In Elizabeth's eyes they had committed treason and should suffer some form of punishment, in fact they should be grateful their heads were still on their shoulders.

Many historians believe Elizabeth's treatment of Katherine was overly harsh and that it was powered by pure jealousy. The queen stood accused of being envious of the beautiful Katherine and her healthy young sons, all of whom were well supported and a threat to her sovereignty. But on the flip side to that we have to accept that Katherine had broken the rules by marrying without the monarch's agreement. She also knew the queen had not favoured her even before her marriage, so what did she expect Elizabeth to do? But perhaps if Elizabeth had been a bit more sympathetic towards Katherine she may not have felt so threatened. Keeping her locked away only served to heighten people's sympathy for her.

As the years passed Katherine's despair grew. It was clear there would be no forgiveness forthcoming from the queen and when she was moved again in September 1567 following Wentworth's death, all seemed lost. Her next home was to be Cockfield Hall and the home of Sir Owen Hopton. Sadly, this was to be Katherine's last move as she died there on 27 January 1568 aged just 27 years old. She was buried at Yoxford church, Suffolk, on 21 February before being reinterred alongside her husband at Salisbury Cathedral following his death in 1621. Her cause of death has often been debated, with the modern theory being that she starved herself to death over her anguish at the separation from her husband and son. The other theory is that she died of consumption (TB) which had led to dramatic weight loss. Either way, Katherine's death was a tragedy for Hertford and their sons – and of course the romantics among us will believe Katherine died of a broken heart, unable to live any longer without her true love. With Katherine now dead, her younger sister Mary stepped into her shoes to become a potential heir, although the Grey curse would haunt her too.

Lady Mary Grey

In 1565, the court was in a flutter when news reached London that Lord Darnley was to marry Mary, Queen of Scots, uniting two of Elizabeth's potential heirs, this news sent Elizabeth into a tailspin and led to the rearrest and imprisonment of Darnley's mother, Margaret. But once again the Grey sisters were in trouble when the youngest,

Mary, aged 20, married without Elizabeth's consent. Mary had clearly not learnt the lesson of her elder sisters when she married Thomas Keyes on 16 July at Westminster Palace. Had Katherine tried to warn her against such folly, or had she in fact encouraged her younger sister to follow her heart and hope for the best? There is even the possibility the two sisters had no contact with each other, Katherine was technically a prisoner and her correspondence would more than likely have been vetted.

Like Katherine and Hertford, Mary and Thomas waited for the queen to be away from court at the wedding of her kinsman, Sir Henry Knollys, before having the ceremony take place. Thomas Keyes was the queen's sergeant porter and had been described as the tallest man at court at 6ft 8 inches, while Mary was the shortest woman due to a spinal deformity she had suffered from birth. As one can imagine, Elizabeth was furious when she heard the news, claiming: 'I'll have no little bastard Keyes laying claim to my throne.' This indicates she must have considered Mary a potential claimant.

Following the clandestine marriage, the couple were interrogated. Mary had learnt something from Katherine's mistakes and had at least three witnesses to her marriage ceremony, but sadly it did not help their cause. The findings of the interrogations resulted in Keyes being sent into solitary confinement at the Fleet Prison, while Mary found herself passed from one family to another, each being a reluctant custodian. First, she was sent to Chequers under the watchful eye of William Hawtry, where she was to stay for around two years. Then, in August 1567, she was placed into the custody of her step-grandmother Katherine Willoughby, the former Duchess of Suffolk. Like her sister Katherine, Mary had little in the way of money and suitable attire so the duchess wrote to Cecil requesting Mary be provided with the necessary means for a lady of her station – that being a potential future queen. Mary stayed with Katherine for two years before again being moved on, this time she went to the home of Sir Thomas Gresham and his family at their home in Bishopsgate and their country seat at Osterly. The Gresham family did not welcome

Mary with open arms, in fact they hated and resented her being among them, seeing her as nothing but a burden. The behaviour of the Gresham family is quite interesting and can tell us how seriously Mary was considered as a potential heir to the throne. If her claim was a serious one, then the family would surely have treated her with respect – after all, you would not want to upset your future monarch. So, from this can we deduce that Mary was never truly considered to be an heir? She doesn't seem to have been taken seriously by anyone; not many records survive about her life and she seems to have been overlooked throughout her life. She was the least beautiful and least intelligent of the Grey sisters, and her deformity may have held her back from ever really reaching the same level of popularity that Katherine had enjoyed. In 1569, after continuously pleading for his release, Thomas Keyes was finally freed from prison and returned home to his children in Kent. He never fully regained his health, or Elizabeth's pardon, but he was reappointed captain of Sandgate Castle where he requested to be allowed to live with his wife; the plea was declined and Keyes never saw Mary again. He suffered bouts of ill health following his release and sadly passed away on 3 September 1571. Following his death Mary pleaded with Elizabeth to be allowed to raise her husband's children, this request was also declined.

In the May of 1572 Mary was finally released from her house arrest but had no friends to turn to and no private income with which to support herself; she was, in effect, destitute. When she left the Greshams, she went to live her stepfather Adrian Stokes and his new wife Anne Carew at their home in Leicestershire. After years of being passed from pillar to post, saving every penny she could, she finally had the means with which to establish her own household in London, and by 1577 she managed to achieve something neither of her sisters had – royal forgiveness. Queen Elizabeth made her one of her maids on honour and Mary served her cousin diligently. Lady Mary Grey died on her 33rd birthday on 20 April 1578 and was buried alongside her mother in Westminster Abbey. Elizabeth did afford Mary a grand funeral with Susan Bertie, Countess of Kent and daughter of

Katherine Willoughby, as chief mourner. Despite Katherine's strong claims to the throne Mary never seemed able to emulate them and so is never really discussed as a potential queen of England, neither did Mary seem to push her claim. None of the courtiers who supported her sister backed Mary, and without that, she stood no chance of mounting an actual claim. With the death of Katherine and Mary, the Suffolk claim for the throne of Elizabeth I came to an end. We will look at the claim of Lord Beauchamp later, but for now there was a Brandon cousin ready to step into the role of potential heir to the throne of England.

Chapter Three

The Clifford Claim

The Clifford claim to the throne came from Eleanor Brandon and down to her daughter, Margaret. As a prominent northern family, the Cliffords were loyal to the crown and would have been proud of their link to the Tudor royal family. When Charles Brandon approached the Earl of Cumberland to discuss a potential marriage between his daughter Eleanor and Cumberland's son Henry, the earl would have found the proposal too good an offer to turn down. Brandon only chose the very best families for his daughters to marry into, so the fact that he chose the Cliffords speaks volumes about how well respected they were.

But was the Clifford claim ever really that viable? Once the Grey sisters had passed away, they most certainly were taken seriously as candidates.

Lady Eleanor Brandon

Eleanor Brandon was the second daughter of Charles Brandon, Duke of Suffolk, and his wife Mary Tudor, Dowager Queen of France and Duchess of Suffolk. She was born sometime in 1519 at the family home of Westhorpe Hall, Suffolk. She enjoyed a relatively carefree childhood and would have spent little time at court given that her mother and father had been banished following their clandestine wedding in 1515. Charles did return, but only after Henry VIII had imposed a large fine on the couple, meaning Mary could not afford to reside at court. She also stood in opposition to her brother Henry over his treatment of Katherine of Aragon while trying to seek a divorce from her in order to marry Anne Boleyn.

Like her elder sister Frances, Eleanor would be found a suitable husband to match her royal status. In March 1535, she married Henry Clifford, the son and heir of Henry Clifford, 1st Earl of Cumberland. The couple were married in June 1535 at the church of St Mary Overies in the presence of her uncle, Henry VIII. Clifford was described as being tall and lean with dark hair; he was well educated, as any man of his standing would be, and when he was younger, he joined the household of Henry Fitzroy, the Duke of Richmond and Somerset and the illegitimate son of Henry VIII, which made him a cousin of Eleanor. Henry was made a Knight of the Bath at the coronation of Anne Boleyn, which established him as a man of importance and therefore a suitable match for the king's niece.

Following the marriage Eleanor left her home and family in London and moved with her husband to the Clifford family seat at Skipton Castle in North Yorkshire, which her father-in-law had renovated in celebration of the marriage. He added two new towers along with a brand-new gallery built for his son and his royal bride. Although the Cliffords were a wealthy prominent family in the north of England, marriage into the royal family brought them prestige. It was a huge coup to have the king's niece residing at Skipton Castle and Cumberland wanted to make sure she was accommodated as befitted her rank.

The north of England had long been a hotbed of rebellion, and Yorkshire was the seat of the religious uprising of October 1536 known as the Pilgrimage of Grace. The leader was Catholic Yorkshireman Robert Aske, and the unrest soon spread across the north to Lancashire, Cumberland and Westmoreland. Aske was a lawyer with good connections – in fact his mother was Elizabeth Clifford, which meant the 2nd Earl of Cumberland, Eleanor's father-in-law, was Aske's cousin once removed. Being a devout Catholic, Aske was dismayed by Henry VIII's sweeping religious reforms, especially the Dissolution of the Monasteries, a reform overseen by Thomas Cromwell. When a revolt took place in York, Aske joined their cause and quickly became their leader.

He was successful in York, managing to drive out the king's tenants from their newly acquired religious homes and return them to the nuns and monks to whom they rightly belonged. In the November of 1536 Aske negotiated with a royal delegation including Thomas Howard, 3rd Duke of Norfolk, and they assured him safe passage to London to speak directly with the king. He met with Henry VIII in London where he gave the king a list of grievances; Henry gave his assurances that Aske's requests would be considered and he was given a safe passage back to Yorkshire. Before he had even left London more fighting had broken out in the North and Henry quickly changed his mind. He had Aske arrested and sent to the Tower to await trial. Aske was charged with, and found guilty of, high treason at his trial at the Palace of Westminster; he was sent back to York, where he was executed outside Clifford's Tower on 12 July 1537.

In order for the revolt to work Aske knew he needed the backing of the northern lords and the Clifford family found themselves in immediate danger because Cumberland and his son refrained from joining the cause. The rebels quickly surrounded Skipton Castle as reinforcements were called for from Carlisle to defend the stronghold and the family within. Eleanor and her infant son were sent to nearby Bolton Abbey with her sister-in-law and attendants for safety. Skipton managed to hold its own, but when the rebels heard Eleanor and her son were at Bolton Abbey, they switched their attention there and managed to breach the walls and take Eleanor and her young son captive. This sent Cumberland into a rage; not only was she his daughter-in-law, but she was the niece of the king and should have been treated with more respect. For the rebels, however, she was a prime prisoner and not one they would be willing to give up lightly. From Cumberland's perspective, he had also failed in keeping his daughter-in-law and grandson safe and surely felt a certain amount of embarrassment at that, not to mention the anxiety over any repercussions that may come from the king. The rebels made their demands. They wanted Skipton Castle and if their demands were not met then Eleanor and her female companions would be handed over to men who would have no regard for their status. Cumberland left for Bolton Abbey immediately to negotiate terms. He was successful, all the hostages were released and the rebels left Skipton within days.

In 1542, the Earl of Cumberland died and Henry and Eleanor became the new Earl and Countess of Cumberland, spending the majority of their time at either Skipton Castle in Yorkshire or Brougham Castle in what is now Cumbria. Sadly, their two sons Henry and Charles died young, not long after their grandfather. Despite this loss, their marriage appeared to be a happy one and the couple were left with a daughter, Margaret, who had been born in 1540. When Charles Brandon died in 1545, he left his daughter jewels and plate worth £200 (approximately £85,000 today). She also received regular gifts from her uncle, the king, with whom she seemed to enjoy a close relationship with. He requested she be the chief mourner at the funeral of Katherine of Aragon in Peterborough Cathedral in January 1536.

Details of Eleanor's life are scant but there is one letter that does survive which gives us an insight into her marriage with Henry. The tone of the letter is loving and warm, and in it she mentions that she is unwell and requests her husband send his doctor to her, it reads:

> Dear heart,
> After my most hearty commendations, this shall be to certify you that since your departure from me I have been very sick and at this present my water is very red, whereby I suppose I have the jaundice and the ague both, for I have none abide [no appetite for] meat and I have such pains in my side and towards my back as I had at Brougham, where it began with me first. Wherefore I desire you to help me to a physician and that this bearer my bring him with him, for now in the beginning I trust I may have good remedy, and

> the longer it is delayed, the worse it will be. Also my sister Powys [Anne Brandon] is come to me and very desirous to see you, which I trust shall be the sooner at this time, and thus Jesus send us both health.
>
> At my lodge at Carlton, the 14th of February.
>
> And, dear heart, I pray you send for Dr Stephens, for he knoweth best my complexion for such causes.
>
> By your assured loving wife,
> Eleanor Cumberland

Sadly, Eleanor died on 27 September 1547, aged just 27/28, at Brougham Castle. Her body was taken from there to be buried in Skipton, where she was laid to rest next to her two sons. In the seventeenth century her tomb was disturbed and opened. Inside her coffin her skeleton was described as being in excellent condition. Based on what was seen at the opening, she was described as being tall with fair hair; she had also been earlier described as being pretty with fine eyes. Henry was said to be devastated by the loss of his wife at such a young age and it has been claimed he fainted with shock when he heard the news. He appeared so ill that his men thought he had died from the heartbreak and even began telling people of his death. When he came round it took him some time to regain his strength, in fact he was so weak that his servants reportedly fed him breast milk. By late 1547 he had remarried, to a lady named Anne Dacre, and the couple had three children together including two sons. When he died in 1570, he was laid to rest next to Eleanor in Skipton. Sadly, there is not much evidence to tell us what kind of relationship Eleanor had with her sister, Frances Grey, in their adult years, one can only imagine they remained in contact via letter. They both married and had families and when Eleanor left London, they appear to have naturally drifted apart but there is mention of Eleanor visiting Bradgate in 1546. Eleanor had already passed away when the scandal involving her niece Lady Jane Grey happened, so we cannot glean any insights from that time; we can only assume Eleanor would have remained loyal to Frances when she lost her daughter and husband to the executioner.

Many believed Eleanor had a stronger claim to the throne than Frances, despite being the younger sister. The reason being that at the time of Frances's birth, Charles Brandon's second wife was still alive and some questioned the validity of his marriage with Mary Tudor – although Henry VIII never showed any concern over the legitimacy of either of his nieces. Due to her early death during the reign of Edward VI, Eleanor was never a contender for Elizabeth's throne, but it is through her that her daughter Margaret held a strong claim to the crown.

Lady Margaret Clifford

Born at Brougham Castle in 1540, Margaret Clifford was the sole surviving child of Eleanor and Henry Clifford, the Earl and Countess of Cumberland. Not much is known about her childhood but we may assume it was similar to that of her Grey cousins given they were all great-granddaughters of King Henry VII and his queen, Elizabeth of York. Initially, the Duke of Northumberland had planned for his son Guildford to marry Margaret, but Cumberland immediately rejected this idea. Not to be deterred, Northumberland then made the suggestion that his own younger brother, Andrew Dudley, ought to be the prospective groom for Margaret. Again, Cumberland refused and even got the backing of King Edward to support his rejections; after all, Margaret was his cousin and her marriage would be of dynastic importance.

Her royal blood ensured Margaret a place as a Lady of the Bedchamber to Queen Mary, and in 1555 it was with the queen's approval that she married Lord Strange, the eldest son and heir to the Earl of Derby. The lavish wedding took place at Westminster and was well attended; Mary could not be there due to illness, but her husband, Prince Philip of Spain did attend, along with her cousins Katherine and Mary Grey. Margaret wanted to put on a show; it was evident to her that Queen Mary did not want Elizabeth as her heir, and she could see that the Grey sisters ought to be discounted from the succession due to their father's treason – this meant that Margaret was next in line to the throne under the terms of Henry VIII's will. The marriage united two of the north of England's most powerful families, the Stanleys of Lancashire and the Cliffords of North Yorkshire and Cumberland. Sadly, it was not a happy union and Lord Strange left his wife to her own devices; the couple separated in 1567. Margaret was ambitious, full of her own importance and was keen to remind people of her right to the throne. She lived an extravagant lifestyle, even by the standards of the day.

In 1570, Margaret's father, Henry Clifford, 2nd Earl of Cumberland, died and she became a very wealthy lady. When Lord Derby died in 1572, she and her husband became the Earl and Countess of Derby, which brought more wealth to the Stanley pot. Unsurprisingly, the ever-absent husband suddenly reappeared and claimed he was happy to live with his wife once more. The couple moved to the Stanley seat of Lathom House, near Ormskirk in Lancashire, where they lived a lavish lifestyle. When both Grey sisters died Margaret became a lady of great interest; it was a distinct possibility that she could become Queen of England after Elizabeth.

The Stanleys had four sons, though sadly only two survived to adulthood. Ferdinando, the eldest, was sent to live at the court of Elizabeth I. He was a very handsome young man and one who Elizabeth kept a very close eye on. His mother may have had a claim to the throne but he was her heir and he was male, and that made him a very notable person of interest as he could easily displace his mother in the line of succession if the right people backed his claim.

Lord Derby was in high favour with the queen and when the cracks in his marriage began to appear again in 1578, Margaret suddenly found herself out of favour with Elizabeth. Did Derby want his wife out of the way so his son could become king of England? It is certainly plausible given his dislike of his wife, but if that was the case he would need to come up with a plan to remove her altogether. But she sealed her own fate in August 1579 when she joined forces with Robert Dudley to oppose the potential marriage between Elizabeth and the French Duke of Anjou. Anjou had spent some time with Elizabeth at Greenwich Palace under the cloak of secrecy, but news his of presence somehow managed to leak out. The finger of suspicion fell on Margaret and her supposed accomplice, Dudley's sister-in-law, Anne Russell.

It was around this time that Margaret began to complain of ill health so she employed the services of a Dr William Randall – but he was no ordinary doctor as many believed him to be a wizard. Unsettled by the rumours that Margaret and the doctor were using Dark Arts against her, the ever-paranoid Elizabeth sent spies to Lathom to keep an eye on the magical doctor and his patient. They both stood accused of using horoscopes and magic to predict the queen's death, and despite Margaret claiming he was just her physician and helping her through illness, the doctor and Margaret were both ordered to London. Within just one week of their arrival, Dr Randall had been arrested, tried, and found guilty of treason; he was executed by hanging. Margaret was placed under house arrest and banished from court. She was sent into the custody of a Mr Seckford of Clerkenwell, Elizabeth's Master of Requests. Margaret's correspondence from around this time indicates that Seckford treated her well, but the similarities between Elizabeth's treatment of Margaret, Katherine and Mary is startling. Was this just another ploy to eliminate her rivals? Just like her cousins before her, Margaret remained under close house arrest – despite petitions from Cecil and Francis Walsingham. Elizabeth remained resolute and refused to release Margaret.

In 1594 Margaret's husband, Lord Derby, who had continued to enjoy Elizabeth's good graces and to whom she had granted the coveted position of Lord High Steward of England, died suddenly from pains in his gut. Had he been the victim of Dark Magic? It would appear so, especially when small wax figures that resembled the earl were found at the home of a Dr Hacket. The figures looked ill-treated and were stuck full of pins, all of which were said to be placed in the gut area. Hacket went the same way as Randall and was hanged, but no link to Margaret was ever established. Margaret was granted permission to attend her husband's funeral in Ormskirk, but on her return to London, she immediately went back to Clerkenwell. Following the earl's death Ferdinando became the 5th Earl of Derby and his wife, Anne Spencer, his countess. The couple had three daughters, Anne, Frances and Elizabeth, but sadly Ferdinando was not to hold the title for long. He died suddenly at Lathom Hall on 16 April 1594, after falling sick at his nearby estate of Knowsley in what can only be described as mysterious circumstances.

Many believed he had been another victim of witchcraft after he fell ill with violent stomach pains and vomiting, much like his father before him. Many believed Ferdinando had been poisoned following his involvement in the 'Hesketh Plot' of 1593. Richard Hesketh was a fellow Lancastrian who had fled England to join the exiled Roman Catholics in Flanders. He was a soldier and served under Sir William Stanley for the Spanish forces during the siege of Antwerp. The Stanleys and the Hesketh were long-standing family acquaintances in Lancashire, so when news of the 4th Earl's death reached the Continent, Stanley – with the aid of a Jesuit priest named Fr. Holt – charged Hesketh with taking a message back to England to urge Ferdinando to claim the throne based on his being the great-grandson of Mary Tudor, daughter of Henry VII. Initially Ferdinando showed interest in the plot, but as soon as his mother became aware of it, she urged her son to tell everything he knew to the authorities; she did not want to see her son lose royal favour as she had. Consequently, Ferdinando betrayed Richard Hesketh and his co-conspirators. Hesketh was tried and found guilty of treason and executed on 29 November 1593. As he stood on the scaffold, he told the gathered crowds that he regretted ever meeting Sir William Stanley. He was just 30 years old when he died.

Following Ferdinando's death his younger brother, Lord William, took the title of Earl of Derby, but his eldest daughter Anne, took his place in the line of succession and when Margaret died while still under house arrest in Clerkenwell on 28 September 1596, her granddaughter Anne inherited her place and suddenly became a lady of importance. Margaret was the last of Henry VII's great-grandchildren to die; she was buried at Westminster Abbey. With another of Elizabeth's claimants gone, the options were getting dangerously few.

Lady Anne Stanley

Anne Stanley was born in May 1580 and was the eldest daughter of Ferdinando and Anne, the Earl and Countess of Derby. Her life was one of scandal and intrigue, but up to 1603 she was considered a potential heir to Elizabeth's throne. Anne and her two sisters inherited a considerable fortune when their father died in 1594, but his title was passed to Ferdinando's younger brother William, who became the 6th Earl of Derby. At the time of her father's death Anne was just 14 years old and a suitable husband would need to be sought. It was not until 1607 that she married Grey Brydges, the 5th Baron Chandos of Sudeley. They lived in great opulence at Sudeley Castle and had at least five children together in what seemed a happy marriage. Sadly, Grey Brydges died in 1621, leaving Anne a wealthy widow.

By the time Ferdinando died, it was clear that Queen Elizabeth was never going to marry and produce an heir of her own. The Stanleys had enjoyed royal favour from the moment Thomas Stanley married Margaret Beaufort and became stepfather to Henry VII, so the focus shifted to Anne as a potential claimant for the crown. But it was her marriage to Mervyn Tuchet, 2nd Earl of Castlehaven, that caused a scandal so great that her name is very rarely linked to the throne. When the couple married in 1624, they were both widowed and it was considered to be a controversial match because Mervyn was more than ten years younger than Anne and had at one time shown Catholic leanings. He was deemed to be beneath Anne in status because his title came from the Irish peerage and considered inferior in England. However, Mervyn was very wealthy and that appealed to Anne, so the couple took up residence at Fonthill Gifford in the South of England.

The Castlehaven family were engulfed in scandal. In 1630 Castlehaven's son from his first marriage, Lord Audley, accused his father of trying to disinherit him. Sometime before 1630 Lord Audley had married Elizabeth – Anne's eldest daughter from her marriage to Grey Brydges – in a bid to keep the family wealth closely tied together. The marriage failed and Audley left Fonthill Gifford, leaving Elizabeth behind. Audley alleged to the Privy Council that Castlehaven had urged Elizabeth (his daughter-in-law and step-daughter) to have sex with a servant named Henry Skipwith, with the resultant child (who would be considered Audley's child) becoming Castlehaven's heir. Audley also accused Anne of taking servants as her lovers. Serious allegations like this needed to be investigated, so the Privy Council interviewed members of the household and Elizabeth – who confirmed she had been made to have sexual relations with Skipwith. She also disclosed that her mother had been raped by servants on the orders of Castlehaven. Castlehaven believed that as his wife he had complete control over Anne's body and could with her as he pleased. After Anne had refused many times to have sex with other men, it is alleged Castlehaven restrained his wife while another man raped her. He was also accused of sodomy with two members of the household but for this he was found not guilty. Lord Castlehaven was arrested, tried and found guilty on a charge of rape. He was executed on Tower Hill on 14 May 1631. It is a story that takes place after Elizabeth I's death, but worth telling I feel as it is an early example of spousal rights and a wife's right to give evidence against her husband in a court of law.

The focus on Anne did not last long and quickly shifted northwards to Scotland and King James VI. It was clear that a male heir was preferred, even if that meant going against the wishes of Henry VIII, whose will stipulated that the Scottish line was to be discounted. If his wishes had been followed, then Anne was the legitimate claimant but she didn't push her claim and never seemed interested in becoming queen, whether that was down to her own personal wishes or the knowledge that she had very little backing. Regardless, the Stanley claim came to an end with Anne and so now the focus switched to those north of the border, whose dynastic right was far stronger than any of those discussed above.

Chapter Four

The Scottish Claim

As previously mentioned, the last will of King Henry VIII stipulated that the crown of England should not pass down the line of his elder sister Margaret due to their Scottish descent. Rules at the time forbade anyone from claiming the throne of England if they had not been born inside the realm. However, one person who fell outside of those rules was Lady Margaret Douglas. She was the daughter of Archibald Douglas, 6th Earl of Angus, and Margaret Tudor. Due to tensions with the Scottish council Margaret Tudor fled Scotland whilsy heavily pregnant and gave birth to her daughter at Harbottle Castle in, Northumbria. Margaret Douglas is said to have shared a close relationship with her uncle, King Henry and was a lifelong friend of Queen Mary. She had been sent by her father to be brought up at the English court as he was at odds with his former wife, and her son, King James V of Scotland, who both wanted Margaret back in Scotland. It was not all plain sailing though and Margaret did cross paths with Henry once or twice over her alleged love affairs, including a dalliance with Anne Boleyn's uncle, Lord Thomas Howard. This came around the time of Anne Boleyn's fall from grace and Henry sent his niece to the Tower over the illicit love affair, although there was never any suggestion that Margaret was complicit in Anne's downfall. It took time, but Henry eventually forgave her and she returned to his favour.

When she married Matthew Stewart, the Earl of Lennox, Henry was very generous in gifting his niece vast lands in the north of England. So why did Henry choose to overlook her as a possible claimant and prefer the Brandon sisters instead? First and foremost, she was a

Catholic, a trait that on more than one occasion would prevent her from being considered a serious candidate. Second, Henry did not wish to see her husband on the throne as king. With his links to both Scotland and France, Lennox was useful to Henry (and would later be of help to Elizabeth for keeping the peace in Scotland) but Henry never once considered him kingly material. The closest Margaret ever got to being genuinely considered the heir was during the reign of Queen Mary, when she put forward her request that should Mary remain childless, Margaret would become queen. Sadly, for Margaret this was never ratified by parliament and Elizabeth became the next queen of England. But that is not to say that Margaret was without influence, and she certainly held sway at court. She was a constant thorn in Elizabeth's side, but Margaret had a weapon more powerful than she ever was: her son, Henry Stuart, Lord Darnley.

Henry Stuart, Lord Darnley

Henry Stuart was born in 1546, although his exact date of birth is unknown. It is widely believed he was born at his parents' northern seat of Temple Newsam, which sits just to the east of the city of Leeds. He was the surviving eldest son of Matthew Stewart, 4th Earl of Lennox, and Margaret Douglas, daughter of Margaret Tudor, her Henry VIII stood as godfather to his young namesake and he was cousin to the three Tudor monarchs that followed him. Darnley was a great-great-great-grandson of King James II of Scotland and a great-grandson of King Henry VII of England, his dynastic pedigree meant that he had valid claims to both the Scottish and English thrones. Matthew Stewart and his younger brother John were sent to France by their mother and into the care of Robert Stewart, 5th Lord of Aubigny; here they enjoyed a rich education and military training, becoming members of the Garde Ecossaise (the Scottish bodyguard to the French King). The English had been keen to marry the young Mary, Queen of Scots, to Prince Edward thereby uniting the two thrones but many Scots were against the match, but Lennox was on the side of the English. It was during this that time he married Margaret Douglas, with the blessing of Henry VIII who attended the wedding with his queen, Katherine Parr. Rules at the time stipulated that in order to claim the throne you had to be born within the realm, and thanks to her mother's panicked flight from Scotland, Margaret fulfilled this criterion making her a very valuable commodity in the marriage market. It proved to be a happy marriage; although the couple suffered greatly with the loss of six of their eight children and spent much time apart. One thing they were united in was their grand ambitions for their eldest son.

Darnley is described as being tall, lean and athletic with very pleasing looks. His parents set about preparing him for greatness from a very young age, educating him well by appointing tutors John Elder, who taught Latin, and John Lallart, who instructed him in French. Darnley could joust, had great swordsmanship and showed a talent for sport, including hawking and horsemanship, and enjoyed the thrill of the hunt. Unfortunately, Darnley was spoiled by everyone around him, which led to his maturing into an arrogant and unlikeable young man.

The Lennoxes were an ambitious family; the earl had a claim on the Scottish throne and Margaret had a claim on the English one, making them both powerful and dangerous. Margaret was especially ambitious for her son, and as a Roman Catholic, she was all the more dangerous to Elizabeth as she could muster support from Catholic countries such as the all-powerful Spain. This put the English Protestants on alert and made the ever-paranoid Elizabeth even more wary than normal, causing her to neither trust nor like her Tudor cousin. Temple Newsam became a hotbed of Catholicism in the north of England and in order to nip any potential rebellion in the bud Elizabeth sent out her league of spies to keep a close eye on the Lennoxes, especially when news reached England from France that Queen Mary had been widowed following the death of her husband, King Francois II. Darnley had met Mary upon the succession of her young husband to the French throne in 1559, he had been sent to

France to offer his congratulations on behalf of his family and to try to persuade Mary to reinstate the Lennox lands to his father. He was unsuccessful, but did receive 1,000 crowns and an offer to attend the coronation. His paths would cross with Mary again just over a year later, when he was sent to offer his family's condolences on the death of Francois; of course he was sent to make a favourable impression on the Scottish queen in the hope that when she was ready to marry again, she may remember her English cousin.

Darnley's pedigree was a hot topic of conversation at the English court, there was a distinct fear that the Catholics would rise up, with a view of putting Darnley on Elizabeth's throne. In fear of this, Elizabeth put the entire Lennox family under arrest. Her fears were not unfounded though as news filtered through that a Catholic spy named Francis Yaxley had been discovered in Lady Margaret's household. Under interrogations at the Tower, Yaxley confirmed the purpose of his mission was to facilitate a marriage between young Darnley and Mary, Queen of Scots, although Mary was unaware at this stage of any plot that involved her marriage to anyone. Mary and Elizabeth's relationship was not an easy one, Elizabeth was wary of her and saw her beautiful Scottish cousin as a threat to her queenship, so the idea she might marry Darnley, one of her own subjects, and seize her throne was very real to her. Despite her fears, Elizabeth refused to condemn any member of the Lennox family; they were her family and, given their popularity in the north, it would have been a dangerous track to go down. Also, to Elizabeth, Darnley was a very realistic choice for her successor, so she warmly welcomed him and his mother back to court – although the presence of the Earl of Lennox was not wanted at that time.

Mary's marriage was the subject of gossip on both sides of the border. She arrived back in Scotland on 19 August 1561. Arriving at Leith after an uneventful journey, the young queen came home to a very different realm from the one she left as a 6-year-old girl. Initially, her nobles were keen to please their captivating young queen, but as a female Catholic in an ever-growing Protestant country, they soon found themselves opposed to her rule. Mary did not understand the volatile nature of the politics in Scotland and so decided to do the one thing Elizabeth had not – she chose to marry, in the hope she might regain some respect from her ministers and provide Scotland with an heir. The fact that Mary felt she had no choice but to marry gives us a good indication of the political state of each country. England was relatively calm; it had had its religious upheavals like most European countries at that time, but Elizabeth had stabilised the country. Mary, on the other hand, had inherited an unstable country that was prone to bouts of violence and savagery, which was so unlike the surroundings in which she had been brought up in France. In order for her to have strength to rule she needed a husband, a man who could restore some order on her behalf and also – perhaps more crucially – a man who could provide her with a male heir. Any woman, whether a queen or not, who can provide her country with the security of an heir commanded respect.

It was in Elizabeth's interest to delay Mary's marriage for as long as possible – but as she was to soon realise, while she was happy to remain unmarried, that did not apply to everyone, and she had little power to interfere. In 1563, Elizabeth had suggested to Mary's secretary William Maitland that Mary ought to take Robert Dudley as her husband, an idea that fell instantly flat with the Scottish Secretary of State. He considered that, from Mary's point of view, Dudley was far too beneath her in status to ever be considered. Dudley may have been Elizabeth's favourite but he held no title, and the suspicion surrounding his wife's death and his other adulterous affairs was certainly not something Mary would want to deal with. What was Elizabeth's plan here? Was she being dismissive of Mary by offering her a man she herself had declined to marry, or was she putting Mary in her place and reminding her that she was the queen of England, not her? Or was this something else entirely? As historian Anne Somerset suggests in her book *Elizabeth I*, did she see this as a way of rewarding and honouring Dudley for his loyal service to her by offering him a queen to marry? But Dudley's affection for Elizabeth was far greater than any feelings he had, or may have had, for a future wife – or so Elizabeth hoped. She hoped he could influence Mary enough for her to stop the insistent demands that she be named as heir presumptive to the throne of England, and there was also the advantage that Dudley could become a spy for England.

Maitland refused to even mention Dudley's name to Mary on his return to Scotland, but Elizabeth was insistent on pressing Dudley's suit and instructed her minister, Thomas Randolph, to take the matter further. It fell to him to advise Mary that if she married an Englishman of Elizabeth's choosing then she would pretty much be guaranteed the English throne when Elizabeth died. When the identity of the suitor was revealed, it did not go down very well with the Scottish queen. Mary was aghast and insulted that Elizabeth had suggested she marry a mere subject; Elizabeth was forever talking about princely virtues and the right of kings, and yet here she was offering Dudley to a fellow monarch. Surprisingly, though Mary did not discount Dudley, she just did not talk of it again, especially as she was conducting her own negotiations elsewhere. When in London, Maitland had made discreet enquiries with the Spanish Ambassador Alvaro de la Quadra over a potential match between Philip II's eldest son, Don Carlos, and Mary. A match that would have sent shivers down England's spine. Elizabeth advised Maitland that should Mary make such a match then her chances of claiming the English throne would be severely hampered. Elizabeth acted by creating Dudley the Earl of Leicester on 29 September 1564 in a ceremony at Westminster Hall.

In a surprise move, Cecil urged Elizabeth to send Lord Darnley north to Scotland, which seems a rather odd decision given the English were still trying to press for a marriage with Dudley. Yes, this was a huge risk on their part, but Cecil was confident that Mary would seek Elizabeth's approval before marrying the 19-year-old Darnley. In another surprising twist, Dudley, now Earl of Leicester, also backed Cecil in this plan as he had no desire to go to Scotland to marry the queen; all he wanted was to remain by Elizabeth's side and serve her as best he could. What neither Cecil nor Leicester realised was that Mary would marry Darnley regardless of what Elizabeth said, and by doing so they would create a formidable pair.

On 3 February 1565, Darnley left London with the permission of Queen Elizabeth. He was to travel to Scotland to accompany his father, the newly restored Earl of Lennox, who had returned home earlier also with the blessing of Elizabeth, home to England. Under no circumstances were they to stay longer than three months and Darnley was certainly not authorised to enter into a marriage with the Scottish queen, but of course that was the plan all along. He arrived in Edinburgh on 12 February, and on the 17th, he was presented to Mary at Wemyss Castle in Fife. The queen was said to be taken with her English cousin, his good looks seemed to have won her over and soon there was talk of marriage on both sides of the border. Darnley accompanied the queen back to Holyrood at the end of February and it appeared to everyone the couple were smitten with one another and were rarely out of each other's company.

Mary sent her trusted advisor, Sir James Melville, to London to discuss the marriage and seek her approval for the match but Elizabeth was horrified. In response, she sent Nicholas Throckmorton to Scotland to put an end to all talk of a marriage between the pair and to tell Mary she could have the pick of any English nobleman to marry – except Lord Darnley. Elizabeth remained confident that Mary would never marry against her wishes, but if she did insist on marrying Darnley then she had to accept she would never inherit the English throne. The one thing that no one took into consideration was just how hopelessly in love Mary had fallen with the attractive young Englishman.

When news reached London of the union between Mary and Darnley, the Privy Council knew they had to act to try to calm the situation down. In order to show Mary and Darnley they were not Elizabeth's automatic heirs, the Privy Council decided to push the suit of Katherine Grey. Although Katherine was under house arrest at the time, it was decided to relax restrictions against her in a bid to show Mary and Darnley that Katherine was still there to take the throne – and in fact had the greater claim under Henry's will. We know how Katherine's story ends, but at this precise time she became a person of huge importance once again. Elizabeth was not happy, however, she did not like Katherine and felt betrayed by Mary, whose actions seemed calculated; Mary knew how Elizabeth would take the news of her marriage to Darnley and carried on regardless.

Elizabeth ordered Darnley and his father home but they defied her orders. On 22 July 1565, Mary created Darnley the Duke of Albany, a sure sign that the marriage was impending. The marriage banns were read in Holyrood Abbey and it looked like nothing could stop this wedding from taking place, not even the queen of England. As punishment, Elizabeth arrested and imprisoned Darnley's mother, Margaret Douglas, in the Tower of London. This marriage had been Margaret's ambition, so perhaps the prospect of her son on the throne of Scotland was worth her time in the Tower; it was not the first time she had been held prisoner there, and she was held in some comfort. Lord Darnley and Mary, Queen of Scots, were married early morning on 29 July 1565 in a Catholic ceremony inside a private chapel at Holyrood, this was followed by a nuptial mass which the groom chose not to attend. Despite his mother's devotion to the Catholic faith, Darnley was never truly affiliated with one religion; he was born and raised as per his mother's faith but later developed leanings towards Protestantism, which would have made him an extremely popular choice for king of England. It would also mean he fitted well into the ever-changing religious landscape of Scotland, unlike Mary, who was unwavering in her dedication to the Catholic faith.

Up to now, Darnley had been the ever considerate and devoted partner to Mary, but it was not long after the wedding that his true personality began to show. Mary soon saw what a vain and arrogant man she had married. He appeared to be the complete opposite of how he had portrayed himself; had he been performing a role in order to snare Mary into marriage? His temperament was veering towards violence, especially when drunk – which happened to be most days and nights; he had become petulant and childish and quickly became a liability to the country. He had never been popular in Scotland and soon enough he became so disliked among the nobles and Mary's councillors that he found himself isolated. But what was Darnley's problem? He had just married the beautiful Mary Stewart, Queen of Scotland, and yet his behaviour was of someone who had been dealt a life blow. It quickly became clear Darnley was not content with the title of King Consort, he wanted the Crown Matrimonial. But Mary refused to give it. The Crown Matrimonial was initially sought by Mary's first husband, King Francois I of France and the Scottish Parliament. If granted it would have made Francois co-ruler of Scotland, and in the event of Mary dying before Francois and without issue, he would have retained the Scottish throne. It would also have allowed the Scottish throne to be passed to any future children Francois may have had with another wife. In essence it would the crown away from Scotland and place it firmly with France. In the end, the Protestants rose up and opposed it and Francois died only a year into his marriage with Mary so this controversial idea was never realised. Now Darnley was married to Mary and he too was demanding the Crown Matrimonial be conferred on him. He felt it was his automatic right as Mary's husband that he be crowned king, but he failed to realise that his erratic behaviour was damaging his chances. There was no way Mary was going to grant his wishes while he was behaving badly.

Despite the shaky start to their marriage, Mary soon fell pregnant with the couple's first child. But that news did nothing for marital relations and the troubles only got worse. On 9 March 1566, Mary's private secretary David Rizzio was murdered in front of her, supposedly on the orders of her husband. The queen was taking supper in her private rooms at Holyrood with a few of her ladies when a group of rebel lords burst into the chamber demanding Rizzio be handed over to them. As the events unfolded, he cowered behind the queen's skirts, begging her to protect him, but when a pistol was aimed at her pregnant belly, she had no option but to stand aside. Rizzio was then dragged from the room before being stabbed multiple times and flung down a staircase. As his lifeless, mutilated body lay at the foot of the stairs, he was stripped naked of his fine clothes and jewels before being buried in the cemetery of Holyrood Abbey. Mary would later see that his remains were reinterred in the tomb of kings of Scotland within the Abbey. If you visit the Palace of Holyroodhouse in Edinburgh, you can visit the site of Rizzio's murder in the Audience Chamber, where a plaque sits above a red stain on the wooden floor, said to be the blood of Mary's Italian beloved private secretary.

Rizzio had been an unpopular figure; rumours had begun to circulate around court that the Italian was the father of the queen's unborn child and that the attack had been instigated by Darnley in retaliation to his wife's behaviour, and to force her to confer the Crown Matrimonial on him. In reality, Darnley had been duped by the lords; they had promised to back his claim to be king if they gave him access to the queen and Rizzio. It turned out to be an unmitigated disaster for Darnley. He was no longer trusted by his wife and the Lords turned their backs on him, claiming the murder was all his doing and that they were just following his orders – they even implicated him further by leaving his dagger beside Rizzio's blood-soaked body. But Mary, now being held in her rooms as a prisoner by the rebel lords in order to stop her from fleeing Scotland, had no option but to let her husband back in. As much as she hated to admit it, she needed him in order to escape. Over the next two days he managed to convince his wife that the attack was not of his doing and that, with the help of the Earl of Bothwell, they should flee Holyrood and head for the safety of Dunbar Castle. They successfully managed to escape late in the evening of 11–12 March before returning to Edinburgh on 18 March, when Mary made peace with her rebel lords, whom she restored to the council.

On 19 June 1566, Queen Mary gave birth to a son at Edinburgh Castle, he was named James Charles Stuart. When he was baptised on 17 December 1566 at Stirling, Castle, Elizabeth I was named as one of his godparents (represented by Francis Russell, Earl of Bedford). Darnley was still sulking, and despite being at residence in the castle at the time, and much to the disgust of his father, he refused to attend the ceremony. Despite the birth of their son, the marriage still had problems – Darnley was plotting to have her ousted as queen, and she no longer trusted him. Something was going to have to give in the marriage; Darnley was becoming ever more the liability and could not be trusted with state business so he took himself off to his father's Glasgow estates where he could wallow in his own self-pity. While there he fell seriously ill with smallpox (some accounts suggest it may have been the effects of syphilis) and before long, Mary came running to her ailing husband's side. She somehow managed to persuade him to return to Edinburgh with her so that she could help him recover while being closer to the court. She did not, however, want him lodging with her at Holyroodhouse, so she arranged for him to take up residence in a two-story house in Kirk o' Field, which lay just on the outskirts of the city.

During the night of 9–10 February 1567, a huge explosion rang out across the city of Edinburgh. In the early hours of the next morning, Darnley's lifeless body was found next to that of his valet in the garden of the Old Provost's Lodgings in Kirk o' Field, just eight months after the birth of his son. On the evening of the blast Mary had visited Darnley but left him just before midnight as she was to return to Holyrood to join in the marriage celebrations of two of her favourite servants, Sebastian Pagez and Christina Hogg. She had originally agreed to stay the night with her husband and it looked like a full reconciliation had happened but as this was his last night of convalescence, she assured him they would be together the following evening. Before Mary left, she gave Darnley a ring as a token of their reunion; he was said to be disappointed at his wife's departure but the lords that had accompanied her there were keen for her to leave and to return to Holyrood.

At around 2 am, a large explosion rocked Edinburgh, waking its residents from their slumber – including the queen. Investigations the following morning found two empty barrels of gunpowder under the Old Provost's Lodgings, which had been reduced to a pile of rubble, directly under the room in which Lord Darnley had been sleeping. But, surprisingly, he was nowhere to be found within the ruined remains of the building so the search turned to the grounds. After a thorough search of the grounds, the mutilated bodies of Lord Darnley and his valet William Taylor were found at around 5 am in the orchard behind the building. Darnley was dressed only in his nightshirt, which suggests he had been tipped off about the impending blast and had tried to make his escape. But if Darnley had managed to flee the blast, how had his lifeless body come to be found outside in the orchard? When a post-mortem was carried out, it revealed he had suffered internal injuries, including broken ribs, but on the outside of his body there were no visible marks that showed any kind of injury. There was also no gunpowder residue found on his fur-lined cloak or body, all that was found lying next to him was a length of rope, a dagger, and a chair – so he had obviously had time to plan an escape despite his panic.

Upon the discovery of the bodies, a message was sent to Mary to inform her of her husband's death. Her leading nobles, Bothwell, Huntly, Argyll, Maitland and Atholl, rushed to their distressed queen's side to offer comfort. Mary was said to have been appalled by the news and believed herself to be the true target, given that she had been there only a few hours earlier and had made plans to spend the night there.

Bothwell, a man who was going to play a big part in Mary's eventual downfall, was ordered to leave the palace and hunt down those responsible for this heinous crime. The shock of Darnley's death plunged the court into mourning and Mary planned to enter forty days' seclusion, as was the French custom. In the aftermath of Darnley's murder, the Privy Council launched an investigation in the hope the traitors would be apprehended and dealt with.

The early understanding was that Bothwell was behind the plot along with other nobles including Morton, Archibald Douglas and Balfour. It transpired that the warden of the Old Provost's lodgings was a man called Hepburn of Bolton, who happened to be a kinsman of Bothwell and no doubt gave them easy access to the property – he may even have supplied them with their own set of keys for them to come and go as they pleased. According to reports from the time, it was Bothwell who pushed for the use of gunpowder, as Darnley had too many loyal men about him to make stabbing an option, and poisoning would have taken too long; they wanted rid of him, and fast. The other benefit of using explosives is that any incriminating evidence would most likely be destroyed in the blast, wiping out any trace of their involvement – along with Darnley they had hoped. Each man had his role to play and it was said to be Balfour who acquired the gunpowder and oversaw the storage and movement of it into the cellar beneath the lodging. It had been kept in a safe house up to the evening of the blast when it was moved quietly into place.

Everything was set, Darnley was installed in the house, Mary had departed for the evening and the gunpowder was ready to be lit – but something, or someone, must have alerted Darnley to what was afoot in order for him to try to escape. Bothwell must have been perplexed when he discovered Darnley was dead but was not killed directly in the blast. So, what exactly had gone wrong? Had the two men been blown from the building by the sheer force of the blast? Apparently not. It came to light that he and Thomas had managed to scramble atop the town walls adjoining the lodging and from there they were able to lower themselves down using a chair and a length of rope. It is thought he stumbled on landing, causing him to break a rib. Thinking they were free, they then made their way through the south garden, but lying in wait was Archibald Douglas and his men; they had been waiting in cottages and were positioned there to prevent Darnley from leaving. It is said both men were then suffocated. It is thought this murder took place prior to the explosion, but knowing the blast was coming, Douglas and his men had no time to drag the bodies back towards the lodging. Instead, they laid out the bodies next to the chair but rope and when they made their escape, they accidentally left a velvet slipper behind in their hasty retreat back up Blackfriars Wynd and into the city of Edinburgh.

The accusations spread fast and were far-reaching, suspicions grew around anyone with a grudge against Darnley and his family – to be fair, that was pretty much anyone at court. The Lennoxes main rivals at court were the Hamiltons and that meant the Archbishop Hamilton fell under suspicion. Current thinking is that Bothwell was behind the plot to murder Darnley; his name was constantly mentioned when his known associates were questioned under torture. But what about Mary? Did suspicion fall on the queen too? Yes, it was well-known that she and Darnley had been suffering a breakdown of their marriage and she had even discussed with her council the possibility of a divorce, but only stopped short because such an action would render Prince James illegitimate. Many believed that Mary's dash to her husband's sickbed in Glasgow and her subsequent decision to move him to Kirk o' Field to convalesce was nothing more than a ruse on her part. She visited him every day and gave every indication the marriage was back on track, but did she do that to lure him away from his family and into a death trap? Such suspicions arose soon after his death, with many believing Mary and Bothwell had conspired together to kill her husband – and her behaviour following his death did little to dispel the rumours.

She showed very little emotion when visiting his body and did not allow him a state funeral. He may not have been king, but he was of noble stock and was father to the future king, he surely deserved a burial that befitted his station. If the marriage had been back on track, would she not have wished her husband be given a right and proper funeral? Instead, Mary had him interred in the tomb of kings at Holyrood. The lack of a state funeral did not go down well in London; Scotland may have rid itself of a troublesome consort, but in England, Elizabeth had one less heir to choose from. Elizabeth's reaction to Darnley's death was one of shock, and the rumours of Mary's implication had even made their way to London. Elizabeth wrote to Mary on 24 February urging her to do all she could to find the perpetrators of this heinous crime. She told Mary 'preserve your honour', the letter was empty of the usual warmth the two cousins shared and if Mary thought that was harsh, the letter from her former mother-in-law, Catherine de Medici, was brutal and to the point, telling Mary she would be an enemy of France if she failed to bring the culprits to justice. Mary refused to act and more and more placards sprang up across Edinburgh accusing her of being complicit in her husband's murder. All the while, Bothwell remained free.

Elizabeth also wrote to Lennox, who had remained in Scotland following his son's death, and promised to bring to justice those responsible for killing his son. Like Mary, however, she took no immediate action and no official investigation was forthcoming. Despite entering seclusion, Mary did attend the wedding of her loyal servant Margaret Carwood, an action that was heavily criticised. She moved frequently between Edinburgh and Seton and often dined with friends. The damage to her reputation was done; her behaviour following Darnley's death would dog her for years to come, and ultimately contribute to her tragic downfall. In her eyes, her saviour Bothwell was free from all suspicion, but before long pamphlets appeared across Edinburgh openly accusing the pair of the murder and it did not take long for rumours to circulate that the pair were about to marry – despite the fact that Bothwell already had a wife.

With Mary in official mourning, Bothwell became the de facto ruler of Scotland; he was a powerful man and one that Mary needed by her side, but could she really have sanctioned the death of her husband? Granted, they had been entangled in a loveless marriage and she had discovered his plans to remove her from the throne, but regicide was not a crime an anointed monarch would ever consider. Like Elizabeth, Mary believed in the divine right of kings and queens, so to kill a fellow crowned being was a step too far – but for Bothwell, it was a different matter. Mary may have wished to have Darnley out of her life, but death was final and a high-risk strategy. Did she despise the father of her child so much, or did she let her heart rule her head as she is so often accused of doing? The pressure on Mary to act against Bothwell grew so great that in the end she had no option but to give in, although she stopped short of launching an official inquiry. Instead, she allowed Darnley's father, the Earl of Lennox, to bring a private prosecution against Bothwell in parliament. But that in itself was a mockery; as the plaintiff, Lennox, was only permitted to bring six people to the hearing, but as Edinburgh was awash with Bothwell supporters, he did not even dare to step foot inside the capital. Bothwell rode to court on the appointed day flanked by nearly 200 men, needless to say the case was dismissed and as Mary watched on from the upper balcony, she could not have imagined how swift her downfall was going to be.

We will never know just how involved Mary was in the events of 10 February 1567. In 1568, the Casket Letters – a series of letters supposedly between Mary and Bothwell – were produced against her during her incarceration in England and used to prove her guilt (more of these later), but the truth about the Scottish queen's involvement is unlikely to ever be fully understood. Mary needed to distance herself from the scandal if she wanted any chance of succeeding Elizabeth to the English throne and Elizabeth urged her to hold a full and thorough investigation to clear her name, but she refused to take that advice. Surely, she was either complicit or, at the very least, guilty of protecting someone from suspicion. Mary's fate seemed sealed when she married Bothwell just weeks after Darnley's assassination. She lost her son, her throne and her freedom, and when she turned to Elizabeth for help, her rival queen decided to imprison her lest she become a figurehead for English Catholics. But just how close did Mary come to sitting on the English throne?

Mary, Queen of Scots

When James V of Scotland died unexpectedly on 14 December 1542, his 6-day-old daughter Mary Stewart became Queen of Scotland. On 24 November, James's army had suffered a humiliating defeat to the English army at the battle of Solway Moss and, despite his not being on the battlefield, the rout would have been an embarrassment him.

His mother, Margaret Tudor, had died in 1541 and so there was no longer any reason to keep the peace between Scotland and England. James was at Falkland Palace at the time of the battle and was soon taken ill; he died just three weeks later aged 30, having never laid eyes on his daughter and heir, Mary. He lived long enough to know he had left a legitimate heir to sit on the throne of Scotland – it is said that when he heard his wife, Marie de Guise, had given birth to a girl he exclaimed: 'it cam wi' a lass, and it will gang wi' a lass', he then turned his face towards the wall and waited for death to take him from his misery and disappointment.

James was right, the Stewart/Stuart reign would end with a woman – but that woman would be Queen Anne in 1714 and not his daughter. Mary was born at Linlithgow Palace and, due to her young age when she acceded to the throne, Scotland was ruled by a succession of regents – including her heir, James Hamilton, Earl of Arran, a great-grandson of James II. In April 1554, the 11-year-old Mary, now betrothed to Francois, Dauphin of France, was living in on the continent when the post of regent passed to her French mother, Marie de Guise. De Guise looked to her relatives across the channel to help guide her and govern Scotland which found many Frenchmen being given lucrative offices of power. The Scots were content with this as it riled their English neighbours.

Marie's regency was plagued with trouble, especially as the growth of Protestantism swept across Scotland along with an anti-French attitude. Marie could have easily packed her bags and left Scotland and returned to her homeland but she decided to stay and fight to protect her daughter's throne. She saw protecting Mary's crown from anti-Catholicism as doing God's work.

Marie did visit Mary in France in 1550 and she stayed for over a year; the two were able to spend much time together at the lavish French court but when she returned to Scotland she found a country on the verge of destruction. The Protestant offensive was growing stronger and louder with churches being ransacked and monks thrown out of their monasteries leaving Marie appalled and saddened.

Resentment was also growing over the influence the French were having on Scotland and its politics. French nobles held the most covetous positions at court and so were becoming richer, leading them to laud it over their Scottish counterparts and by 1559 Scotland had plunged headlong into utter turmoil. It saw Catholic against Protestant, Scottish against French and clan verses clan – at times there was even discord within the same family; all these arguments brought the country to its knees.

By late 1559, Marie faced all-out rebellion against her regency but she remained courageous and fought off the attack from men like John Knox. Disgruntled, Knox turned towards Elizabeth and England to help rid Scotland of Catholics and the French. While Elizabeth rejected Knox due to his stance on female rulers, she did send an army to assist the Scottish Protestants in expelling the French. Despite the troubles and constant threat to her regency, Marie de Guise never relinquished the role and ensured her daughter's throne remained safe – and Catholic. Marie de Guise died from dropsy (oedema) on 11 June 1560 at Edinburgh Castle, aged 44. Her body lay in state and was placed in St Margaret's Chapel before being secretly shipped back to France in March 1561, where her funeral was held in July, attended by her daughter Mary. The mother and daughter shared a close relationship and Mary would miss her mother's guiding hand when she returned to Scotland following the death of her husband. Would Mary have made the decisions she did if her mother had been there to advise her? Perhaps not. But Mary had grown into her own woman who was to be held responsible for her own actions.

Mary, Queen of Scots, was crowned on 9 September 1543 at Stirling Castle – she had yet to turn 1 year old. Mary was the great-granddaughter of Henry VII of England through her maternal grandmother Margaret Tudor (who coincidentally was also grandmother to Mary's second husband Lord Darnley) and it was this direct link to the Tudors that gave Mary her claim to the English throne. Henry VIII, Mary's great-uncle, had been keen to unite the thrones of England and Scotland and had aimed to do this by

1. *Queen Elizabeth I of England*, Artist Unknown, 1575. (via WikiCommons)

Left: 2. *Mary, Queen of Scots*. (via WikiCommons)

Below left: 3. *King James VI of Scotland and I of England* by John de Crtiz, 1604. (via WikiCommons)

Below right: 4. *Henry Stuart, Lord Darnley*, Artist Unknown, 1564. (via WikiCommons)

Above: 5. *Lady Katherine Grey and her son Lord Beauchamp*. (via WikiCommons)

Right: 6. *Lady Mary Grey* by Hans Eworth. (via WikiCommons)

7. *Lady Arbella Stuart*, Artist Unknown, 1589. (via WikiCommons)

8. *Lady Eleanor Brandon, or, Lady Margaret Clifford* by Hans Eworth. (via WikiCommons)

9. *Ferdinando Stanley, 5th Earl of Derby*, Artist Unknown, 1594. (via WikiCommons)

10. *Anne Stanley, Countess of Castlehaven* by Cornelis Janssens van Ceulen. (via WikiCommons)

11. *Lady Jane Grey*, Artist Unknown. (via WikiCommons)

Right: 12. *King Henry VIII of England*, Hans Holbein the Younger. (via WikiCommons)

Below: 13. *King Edward VI of England*, William Scrots. (via WikiCommons)

14. *Queen Mary I of England*, Master John. (via WikiCommons)

15. *Queen Anna of Denmark*, John de Critz, 1605. (via WikiCommons)

16. *Henry Frederick, Prince of Wales*, Robert Peake the Elder, circa 1610. (via WikiCommons)

17. *Princess Elizabeth Stuart, Queen of Bohemia*, by Marcus Gheeraerts the Younger. (via WikiCommons)

18. *Charles Stuart, Prince of Wales and later King Charles I*, Anthony van Dyck, 1641. (via WikiCommons)

19. *King Francois II of France*, by Francois Clouet, 1558. (via WikiCommons)

20. *James Hepburn, 4th Earl of Bothwell*, Artist Unknown, 1566. (via WikiCommons)

Above left: 21. *James Stewart, 1st Earl of Moray and Regent of Scotland*, by Hans Eworth, 1561. (via WikiCommons)

Above right: 22. *Robert Dudley, 1st Earl of Leicester*, by Steven van Herwijck, circa 1562. (via WikiCommons)

Right: 23. *King Henry VII of England*, Artist Unknown. (via WikiCommons)

Above: 24. *Charles Brandon and Mary Tudor, the Duke and Duchess of Suffolk*, Artist Unknown. (via WikiCommons)

Opposite above: 25. Loch Levan Castle. (via WikiCommons)

Opposite below: 26. *The Murder of David Rizzio*, John Opie, 1787. (via WikiCommons)

27. *King James VI of Scotland as a child*, Artist Unknown, circa 1574. (via WikiCommons)

28. The ruins of Bolton Abbey. (Author's image)

engineering a marriage between his only son and heir Prince Edward and Queen Mary. This arrangement would have meant Mary leaving Scotland for England in order for Henry to oversee her upbringing. When she was just 6 months old, the Treaty of Greenwich was signed which would have facilitated Henry's plans – but would also have guaranteed the two countries would remain separate.

Keen to keep the Auld Alliance between Scotland and France alive, the Scottish nobles declared they were not keen on the idea of handing over their infant queen to England,and pushed for a French allegiance instead. Hoping to reignite the Auld Alliance against the English, in December 1543, the Scottish Parliament officially rejected the Treaty of Greenwich and England's plans, triggering Henry's military campaign that became known as the 'Rough Wooing'. He hoped that by threatening war he could force their hand, but all he succeeded in doing was pushing the Scots closer towards the French. Following a crushing defeat by the English at Pinkie Cleugh on the 10 September 1547, the Scots still refused to come to terms with the English and at that point decided to send their young queen to safety to Inchmahome Priory, before smuggling her out from under the noses of the English and away to France. Henri II was more than happy to come to Scotland's aid and when help arrived the Scottish government wasted no time in agreeing to the marriage between Queen Mary and Francois. Mary sailed to France from Dumbarton on 7 August 1548 where she was to stay for the next thirteen years of her life, she often looked back on those years as the happiest of her life.

In 1548, Mary was betrothed to the Dauphin of France, the future King Francois II. In preparation, she had been sent to France at the age of 5 to be brought up at court in order learn its customs and etiquette, which were far grander than those of the Scottish court. Mary Stewart may have been Queen of Scots, but when the time came, she would also ascend the throne of France alongside her husband, which happened far earlier than expected. Henri II had been king of France since March 1547 when he succeeded his father, Francois I.

He had married Catherine de Medici in 1533 and despite his open relationship with his mistress Diane de Poitiers, the couple managed to have eight children together. By betrothing his son to Mary, he was hoping to build a dynasty that would bring the two kingdoms together under French rule and by doing so, establish a claim to the throne of England through any children Mary and Francois may have.

The young couple were married in Paris in April 1558 in a lavish ceremony that saw the streets around Notre-Dame full with onlookers who wanted to catch a glimpse of the radiant Scottish queen as she married the Dauphin, the first to be wed in Paris in 200 years. Special stages were erected in order to allow as many people to see the day's celebrations as possible. The royal arms of Scotland were embroidered on blue silk alongside the golden fleur-de-lis of France to give the impression of a star-studded sky; the only star the crowd wanted to see, however, was Mary Stewart, a queen in her own right and one who shone brighter than any star in the night sky.

She wore a gown of brilliant white with a grey train and a cloak encrusted with pearls. Around her neck she wore a diamond necklace, possibly the one left to her by her grandmother Margaret Tudor, and on her head a crown, although it was not her regal crown as the Scots would not let their crown jewels leave the country. Mary was the embodiment of regal magnificence and it was easy to see how she had charmed the people of France, they had taken her to their hearts and rejoiced as she arrived at the Cathedral on the arm of their King, and her uncle the Cardinal of Lorraine. Her other uncle, the revered Duc de Guise, was the master of ceremonies and had arrived earlier to much acclaim. The marriage procession was long and included a band of Scottish musicians who were decked out in red and yellow livery in honour of their queen. After them came a host of gentlemen from the king's household who were then followed by the royal princes. Next came the religious men, the bishops, archbishops and finally the cardinals, all decked out in their finery. Finally, before Mary's arrival came the Dauphin himself. Francois looked young for his 14 years and his frailty was clear for all to see – and which became even starker when he took his place beside his glorious bride. When Mary arrived, she looked elegant and although she was only 15 years old, she looked every inch a queen. Her renowned beauty made her stand out; she was tall, about 6ft in fact, and slim, which gave her an air of elegance that made her look regal and graceful. Her complexion was clear, her eyes were bright and her hair was a deep brown. In a show of regal magnificence, the heralds threw gold and silver coins into the crowds which caused a stampede and in the rush, people were trampled on, causing mayhem and panic. The celebratory grand ball that was held that evening was filled with dancing, with the queen of Scotland taking to the floor with the king of France, she danced gracefully as she towered over the king. The dancing and feasting were followed by a series of pageants which had been designed to enthral and enrapture the gathered guests, and with that Mary, Queen of Scots became the Dauphine of France.

The grandeur of the French court was designed to distance them from ordinary people, who saw their royal family as almost God-like beings. Mary's wedding to Francois was an example of this, and this show of magnificence only added to Mary's belief in the divine right of kings (something her grandson Charles would later lose his head over).

In November 1558, Elizabeth ascended the throne of England as per the will of her father Henry VIII, but Catholics across England and Europe felt Mary was the rightful queen of England. They saw the Protestant Elizabeth as a usurper as they did not recognise the marriage between Henry and Anne Boleyn. Ever keen to cause trouble for England, Henri of France championed the claim that his daughter-in-law, Mary was the true queen. He proclaimed Mary and Francois as the king and queen of England in France, and even went as far as quartering the royal arms of England with those of Mary and Francois – an act that did not go down well across the Channel.

On 30 June 1559, just over a year after the grand wedding ceremony of Mary and Francois, Henri held a tournament to celebrate the marriage of his daughter Elisabeth to Philip II of Spain. During a joust, he was fatally wounded as a fragment of his opponent's lance splintered and pierced the king's eye. Despite the best efforts of his surgeons, the damage to the eye and brain was irreversible and the king contracted sepsis. He died in Paris on 10 July 1559, at the age of just 40. His early death put his fragile son and striking daughter-in-law on the throne much earlier than anyone had been anticipating – but as it would turn out, their reign would be shorter than people had hoped.

Francois was just 15 years old when he became king, he had been a sickly child from birth and so was never strong physically or mentally. He was an inexperienced king who left the governing of the country to Mary's Guise uncles, leaving him the time to go hunting in the French countryside around Orleans. It was here that his health deteriorated in November 1560, and on 16 November, he fainted from a severe earache. Mary and his mother, Catherine de Medici, kept a constant vigil at his bedside but it was clear to see the young king was dying. Francois endured an agonising death, with any treatment just causing him more pain and suffering. The infection from his ear spread to his brain and soon delirium set in. He died in Orleans on 5 December 1560, aged just 16; Mary was just three days shy of her eighteenth birthday. Francois and Mary had reigned for just seventeen months and her dreams of a long-reign as queen of the French Empire lay in tatters as her childhood friend, her companion and husband, lay dead. She grieved deeply for Francois, although it appears no one else did. He was succeeded by his 10-year-old brother who became Charles IX, and Catherine de Medici became regent of France; her time for power had finally come. She would be called upon by Mary for assistance in the future, assistance that she would decline to give. Within six months, Mary had lost her mother and her husband; her future looked far from certain. She had gone from being the glittering jewel in France's crown to suddenly having no role or status at the French court. The Scottish queen was in a very vulnerable position, her Guise uncles lost power and left court leaving her without a guiding hand.

After Francois's death Mary found herself alone at the French court and when Catherine de Medici became regent for her son Charles IX many knew she had no choice but to return home to her kingdom of Scotland. She arrived in Leith on 19 August 1561, nine months after her husband's death and thirteen years since she was last in her home country. Mary had left Scotland a young girl at the age of 5, and returned as a young woman of 18, with little experience of ruling. Reality soon set in when she discovered just how unstable and volatile the religious and political situations in Scotland had become. Gone was the glittering French court where she was pampered and petted as the beautiful Dauphine; gone were the dances and feasts where she was lauded as the most beautiful woman in Europe, this was her new reality and in order to survive she had to adapt – and quickly.

Scotland was just like any other country in Europe at the time, it was divided by religion with the Catholics on one side and the Protestants on the other. Mary was a devout Catholic but her half-brother, James, Earl of Moray, led a powerful Protestant faction at court. A member of that group was John Knox, leader of the country's reformation, founder of the Presbyterian Church of Scotland and constant thorn in Mary's side. Knox openly preached against Mary from the pulpit at St Giles's, condemning her for hearing Mass, but Mary remained resolute and proclaimed there would be no change to the country's current religious ideals. This was something many nobles were happy with as it gave Protestants the freedom to worship as they wished, but Knox was a zealot and continued to persecute Mary and her household for their Catholic ways. Mary and Knox clashed continuously over the next few years, she accused him of inciting rebellion among the people, he openly defied her and when she attempted to have him silenced, the nobles backed Knox. He continued to oppose Mary and her religion and in June 1563, Mary summoned Knox to her presence at Holyrood to discuss her proposed marriage to Don Carlos. She asked Knox what business was it of his to interfere in her marriage, she burst into tears and wept heavily; Knox replied that he took no pleasure in seeing her tears but was adamant he would continue to voice his concerns for the good of the country and its people. In 1563, while Mary was away from Edinburgh, a group of rebels forced their way into her private chapel at Holyrood while Mass was being heard and the priest was threatened. The two ringleaders were scheduled for trial in October but Knox leapt to their defence and requested the nobles intervened on their behalf. Mary intercepted a letter and saw this as a treasonable offence. Knox came and defended himself in front of Mary and the Privy Council but he refused to settle the matter peacefully, arguing that no laws had been broken and he had simply acted in his capacity as a minister of the kirk. The councillors voted that he had not committed treason and no punishment should be brought.

In order to keep the peace, Mary tolerated Protestantism and decided to keep Moray as her chief advisor. The Privy Council remained largely the same but only four of the sixteen men were Catholic. Considering her devoutness, it is surprising she did not take the opportunity to revive her council and place more of the lords that were loyal to her in prominent positions. The fact she did not may indicate Mary was ready to turn away from Catholic France and look towards Protestant England, for if she had designs on the throne she would need to please the Protestants over the border. But keeping many Protestants in their positions made Mary vulnerable as it gave them ample opportunities to plot against her, was this an early showing of her inexperience and ruling? Perhaps, but she had no other option for she had to keep her lords happy if she was going to rule with any success.

Mary wanted to be at peace with Elizabeth but she would only enter into negotiations as long as she be named as Elizabeth's heir. If the English queen did not agree then Mary would refuse to sign the Treaty of Edinburgh (see Appendix Three for transcript), which was drawn up to help maintain peace between England, France and Scotland. It was to dissolve the Auld Alliance between Scotland and France and replace it with an Anglo-Scottish alliance instead. Mary wanted the terms to be amended to state that she would not actively chase Elizabeth's throne while she and any of her children were alive, on the condition that she be made the heiress presumptive. Mary dispatched Maitland to the English court to discuss this matter with Elizabeth but her English counterpart was to be disappointed when Maitland divulged that he was not there to discuss the treaty, but rather to discuss the succession.

Speaking candidly with Maitland, Elizabeth explained that she failed to see why Mary was so worried as her claim was far greater than her rivals, she could barely hide her contempt when she discussed her rivals, claiming 'You know them all, alas! What power or force has any of them poor souls?'. She even went on to mention Katherine Grey's pregnancy to him, but declared she was unable to claim the throne given her father's treasonable behaviour. Despite all she had told Maitland, Elizabeth still declined to officially name Mary as her heiress presumptive. It was clear Elizabeth did not want to face up to her own mortality, the last thing she wanted to do was give her rivals any opportunity to remove her and by naming her heir she ran the risk of them becoming a figurehead for a rebellion – and her beautiful cousin was most certainly someone who could stir a rebellion. But it was clear at this point that Mary was her favoured choice and she went on to tell Maitland, 'I for my part know none better, nor that myself would prefer to her'. This is a pretty strong indication as to where Elizabeth's feelings on the matter lay, but there were still issues that were beyond her control. The will of Henry VIII for example, and the fact that Mary was Scottish and not born of the realm of England, were both issues to be discussed in Parliament and Elizabeth would have to respect the government's decisions should they object. That was another convenient way for Elizabeth to defer from officially naming Mary, but she did advise her to be patient and do all she could to endear herself to the English. In short: do not give them any reason to decline your claim.

Mary was settling into life as Scotland's queen but she faced opposition from many sides, as a Catholic and female, life was never going to be easy. Mary's second marriage was widely talked about and as queen she needed to produce an heir in order to ensure the Stuart dynasty continued. After her first marriage ended prematurely the Scottish queen knew she would need to marry well. A husband could offer her protection, but he would need to be someone who would be happy to defer to his wife in all things as his sovereign; she needed a man who was obedient yet strong. Discussions began about a potential husband for Mary; the French were keen to negotiate a union with Archduke Charles of Austria but this was done without the queen's knowledge and she fiercely rejected the idea, was she bitter over their treatment of her following Francois's death? Perhaps she felt they had no right to discuss her marriage when they were so quick to rid themselves of her.

Instead, she turned to Spain and the son of King Philip II, Don Carlos, the Prince of Asturias. Philip rejected this idea but with hindsight this was a good thing for Mary, given that Carlos had many physical and mental problems. He had been born with one leg shorter than the other and a curvature of the spine which led to shoulders being at different heights. His mental instability was a concern to his family and he was imprisoned by his father after showing signs of violence; he died at the age of 23 with his physical and mental conditions being the result of years on inbreeding among the Hapsburgs.

Even Elizabeth had an opinion on who her cousin ought to marry. She wanted Mary to wed an Englishman through whom she could control the Queen of Scots. Surprisingly, the man offered to Mary was Robert Dudley, Elizabeth's favourite. The hope was that the Protestant Dudley would in some way water down Mary's Catholicism – did Elizabeth envisage Mary and Dudley sitting on the throne of England together? She created Dudley the Earl of Leicester in the hope that a title would make him a more suitable candidate for Mary. If that was Elizabeth's aim, it failed as both Mary and Dudley rejected the idea. Dudley had no wish to move to Scotland and even though Elizabeth indicated that if Mary married an Englishman her claim to the throne would be acknowledged, she still declined the offer.

Then came along Henry Stuart, Lord Darnley. The pair first met in 1561, at which time Darnley had made a suitable impression upon the queen and given his Scottish lineage, he had a legitimate claim on the Scottish throne through his father Matthew Stewart, Earl of Lennox. The couple were next introduced at Wemyss Castle, Fife, in 1561 – a meeting engineered by his parents, who were keen for their son to marry the queen. He again made a favourable impression and before long Mary had chosen her next husband; by 29 July 1565, they were married. News of the marriage did not go down well in Scotland or England. Mary's Protestant lords, led by Moray, went into all-out rebellion as they saw the marriage as an indication that Scotland would turn its back on the Reformation and go back to Rome. The rebels met at Glasgow and Argyll to plot their next move. The English provided the rebels with money, which was one thing Mary struggled to find – no one was willing to pawn her jewels until they were put under the threat of imprisonment. Mary and Darnley requested military support to join them in Edinburgh and from there they set out to Glasgow to face the rebels, who had moved on to Hamilton and from there to Edinburgh. As the castle was held for the queen the cannons were turned on the rebels and began to fire. The rebel lords left Edinburgh and headed for Dumfries, all the while Mary's forces were securing the support of St Andrews, Loch Levan and Dundee. Moray never had enough support to really cause Mary a problem; her forces far outnumbered his and the armoury at her back was far superior. The rebellion left Moray with no choice but to flee Scotland and head over the border into England. He had plans to travel to London but Elizabeth wrote to him and told him to turn back, he was not welcome at her court given he had entered into rebellion against his queen. The rebellion against Mary and Darnley's marriage became known as the 'Chaseabout Raid', and marked the point when the marriage started to decline. Without her half-brother Moray on hand to offer support and guidance, Mary had to turn to her other lords for advice.

Elizabeth may have wanted Mary to marry an Englishman but she did not want that man to be Lord Darnley. Any children of Mary and Darnley would have had a combined claim to the throne of both

Scotland and England, and Elizabeth felt threatend by this. Even though she had been instrumental in bringing them together she never wished for them to marry. At the very least she would have expected them to seek her permission given that Darnley was her cousin and an English subject. Elizabeth was not amused and as Darnley and his father were in Scotland, the queen's wrath fell on his mother. She placed Margaret Douglas, Countess of Lennox, under arrest and sent her to the Tower of London where she remained until the dreaded news arrived that her son had been murdered. Margaret tried to convince her cousin that she was not aware her son had plans to marry the Scottish queen, but she was not the kind of mother to have been unaware of her son's plans. There was no doubt in Elizabeth's mind that Margaret was instrumental in Darnley marrying Mary. Six guards and three of her closet women accompanied Margaret up the Thames to Traitor's Gate; as she entered, did her mind cast back to Anne Boleyn, Catherine Howard or Lady Jane Grey? All women of royal status and standing, but that had not been enough to keep their heads on their shoulders. Given her royal blood Margaret was kept in rather salubrious surroundings in the Lieutenant's Lodgings, which overlooked the Tower Green, but she was allowed no visitors and no communication with Scotland; it would be an anxious time for her and all she could do was sit tight and hope that Elizabeth went no further than just imprisonment.

Mary was shocked when she heard the news of her mother-in-law's arrest and sent her Master of Requests, John Hay, to England to negotiate with Elizabeth for her release. As far as Mary was concerned Margaret had done no wrong and as she resided in England, could not be held responsible for events happening in Scotland. But the English queen had planned to use the imprisonment as leverage against her rival. She was hoping to lure Darnley back to England, but what Elizabeth did not know was that Margaret had instructed both Darnley and his father to stay in Scotland at all costs, they had worked too hard for this to fail now. France and Spain also wrote to Elizabeth to demand the release of Margaret but she stood firm and the Countess of Lennox remained her prisoner.

Darnley did everything he needed to do to get Mary to marry him, he behaved impeccably, was attentive to her and supportive but we know from earlier chapters that he was a dubious character, often liable to drunken violent outbursts. The arrogant King Consort of Scotland was to prove a disaster for Mary and her chances of succeeding to the English throne. Mary soon realised she had made a terrible mistake in marrying the tempestuous youth but before long she was pregnant and trapped in a marriage she could not get out of. Mary gave birth to her son, James Charles Stuart, on 19 June 1566 at Edinburgh Castle. His birth ought to have united his warring parents but with Darnley refusing to attend his son's baptism, it seems things were far from settled. When a queen enters the birthing chamber a nation holds its breath for if she should die, as so many women did, the young infant would become monarch from birth, leading to a constitutional crisis. Thankfully Mary survived the birth and returned to queenship almost immediately.

All the while, Darnley was sulking over Mary's reluctance to grant him the Crown Matrimonial, she was still smarting over the murder of Rizzio, in which Darnley had clearly had a hand, and the marriage was on its knees. Mary decided she wanted to free herself from her troublesome husband and met with leading nobles at Craigmillar Castle near Edinburgh; she was hoping a divorce could be obtained but when they advised her that action would illegitimise her son, other ideas had to be found. Had Darnley got word that his life was in danger? It would seem so as he left Edinburgh and headed to his father's estates near Glasgow but it was during this journey that he fell ill, more than likely with smallpox or syphilis, but perhaps the nobles had got to him before he left and poisoned him.

Regardless of the nature of Darnley's ailment he remained seriously ill for some time. Surprisingly, Mary showed concern at her husband's illness and visited him in Glasgow to nurse him, she managed to persuade him to return to Edinburgh but before long he was dead following an explosion at his lodgings at Kirk o' Field. As we have already discussed, suspicion quickly fell on Mary's favourite, Lord Bothwell; he had been ingratiating himself with Mary over the preceding months and had made himself indispensable to the queen. But it was Mary's direct response that brought into question her involvement. Had she conspired with her nobles to murder her husband, the father of her son? Was that the other idea they had discussed at Craigmillar Castle? The blame fell squarely on Bothwell and he stood trial against the Estates of Parliament at the insistence of Darnley's father Lennox. Lennox could not provide any solid evidence against Bothwell and so he was acquitted of all the charges against him. Cleared of murder, Bothwell coerced a number of nobles and church leaders to sign the Ainslie Tavern Bond, which confirmed his innocence of Darnley's murder and that he was the ideal choice of husband for Mary.

Mary travelled to Stirling Castle to visit her son in April 1567, what happened on the 24th, during her return journey to Edinburgh is still not clear. It is alleged that Bothwell and his men abducted the queen and took her to Dunbar Castle where he supposedly raped her. They returned to Edinburgh and on 15 May were married at Holyrood; Mary was to use the excuse that she married him in order to save her reputation because she was pregnant by Bothwell and it was imperative that child was born in wedlock. It does seem a strange affair and it is difficult to know how involved Mary was in this plot. On the face of it, seems to have been orchestrated with her knowledge as it is hard to image the queen could have been abducted so easily given her personal guard, so there must have been some element of cooperation on her part. Perhaps her hand in marriage was his reward for orchestrating the murder of Darnley. Bothwell divorced his wife just twelve days prior to his marriage with the queen making it seem even more like this elaborate plot had been very well planned. Mary may have been under the impression the nobles supported her marriage, but once again things quickly started to unravel. While the Catholic population did not accept the marriage as it had been performed under Protestant rites, the country as a whole condemned it because Mary had married the man who stood accused of murdering her husband.

Trouble was brewing, and when twenty-six nobles, known as confederate lords, rose against Mary and Bothwell at Carberry Hill, things came to a head. Mary soon found herself with few supporters; she negotiated with the lords that she would come quietly if they let Bothwell leave the field without them giving chase. They agreed, and Bothwell was given safe passage from the field and the country while Mary was taken to Edinburgh under armed guard where she was subjected to cruel taunts from the gathered crowds who branded her an adulterer and murderer. The night following her humiliating ride through Edinburgh the queen was taken to Loch Levan Castle, an isolated fortress which sat on an island in the middle of Loch Levan. At some point in the middle of July, Mary miscarried twin boys; on 24 July, she was forced to abdicate her throne in favour of the 1-year-old James. Her gaoler was Sir William Douglas, whose wife Lady Agnes became a constant companion to Mary, staying with her day and night, giving her no respite. Also in the household was Douglas's mother Margaret Erskine, who also happened to be the mother of Moray – making Mary's gaoler her half-brother's half-brother. Lady Margaret worked hard to keep Mary under close scrutiny for Moray, who was made regent on behalf of his young nephew.

Mary endured a torrid time in Loch Levan Castle. She had no idea what her future held and whether her son was safe but on 2 May 1568, ten months after she had arrived, she managed to escape. She was aided by Sir William's brother George, and another young Douglas lad, maybe an illegitimate son named Will. Mary had tried twice before to escape and failed making her determined this time to succeed. In the disguise of a serving maid the queen managed to slip out of the castle gates and down to the shoreline where Will was waiting with a boat ready to row Mary to the mainland. Waiting for her when she landed was George, an attractive young man said to be in love with her. George was true to his word and with him he had horsemen ready to whisk Mary away; hidden in the surrounding hills and under the command of Lord Seton were a number of other men ready and waiting. They escorted Mary to

Seton Castle and from there they rode to Hamilton where she aimed to rally her troops.

When Moray heard of the escape he was dumbfounded and quickly put out the call to arms. He requested any man, loyal to their king, to convene at Glasgow and be ready to fight. William Douglas was said to have been so distressed at Mary's escape that he tried to stab himself with his own dagger, no doubt his half-brother was not best pleased with his efforts either. Elizabeth on the other hand was delighted when she heard the news that Mary had escaped, although her councillors weren't. She hoped Mary would now be able to regain her throne, but little did she know the Scottish queen was about to become her problem. Eleven days after the escape on 13 May, at the village of Langside, just south of Glasgow, Mary's forces came face to face with Moray's who were fighting in the name of her 2-year-old son, King James VI. Mary had managed to raise an army of 6,000 men which, compared to the opposition's total of around 4,000 should have ensured a victory for the queen but after the battle, which only lasted approximately forty-five minutes, saw 150 men die. Mary, who watched from a vantage point upon a hill, turned her horse around and galloped away, heading for Dumfriesshire and the Solway Firth with one destination in mind – England. She knew that to stay in Scotland meant further imprisonment or death, and not wanting to be a prisoner of her own son she managed to escape south to England in the hope that her cousin Elizabeth would come to her aid. She wrote to Elizabeth telling her of her dire situation and her need of assistance, enclosed in the letter was a diamond, a token of friendship that Elizabeth had previously sent to Mary.

Under the cover of darkness on 16 May, and ignoring her advisors, Mary boarded a fishing boat and crossed the Solway Firth into England, landing at the small fishing village of Workington on the Cumbrian coast. She stayed her first night at Workington Hall as guest of honour of the Curwen family before being escorted to Carlisle Castle where, under the governance of Lord Scrope, she could be protected from any Scottish border raids. She had about forty in her company and efforts were made to accommodate them all and to provide Mary with fresh clothes. Having left everything of value in Scotland she was pretty much destitute and reliant on Elizabeth providing a wardrobe to befit a queen.

Mary took a huge political gamble in putting her faith in Elizabeth by assuming the English queen would rush to help her. As she understood it, she was Elizabeth's heir and so would be protected and reinstated to her Scottish throne with the aid of an English army. Mary had clearly misjudged the situation and had not recognised what a difficult position she was placing her cousin in. From the English point of view the council advised Elizabeth to be cautious, Mary's over-inflated ego and the assumption that England would come to her aid needed to be checked. Elizabeth wrote to Mary advising her to be wary of those around her that flatter her, and that she needed to open her eyes to her true situation. The Scottish queen had always been adept at getting her own was through flattery but that would not work on Elizabeth, who warned her not to threaten England with French involvement. Mary retaliated by telling Elizabeth that she had other allies to call upon, so it was clear early on England would not go to war over the state of Mary, Queen of Scots.

Another reason for Elizabeth's delay was her need to understand Mary's involvement in the murder of Darnley, and whether or not she had been unjustly treated by the confederate lords. Until that had been determined Elizabeth refused to meet Mary, who was to remain under close supervision in the north of the country. The north of England had remained predominantly Catholic and had often shown disdain to Westminster, and so when the news of Mary's arrival spread, the northern lords were clamouring to play host to the Scottish queen.

The problem with having Mary in the north was that they could all rise in rebellion to promote the Catholic queen to the English throne, Elizabeth wanted her away from the melting pot of Catholic revolt and so moved her further south and away from the Scottish border. In July 1568, Mary was moved from the grand castle at Carlisle to Bolton Castle in Wensleydale, Yorkshire, as it was seen as a safer option.

She was unhappy about the move and made protests to Elizabeth, demanding she would have to be taken by force, but in reality Mary had lost any right to bargain with Elizabeth, she was in no position to make any demands so in the end she went quietly. Yorkshire and the Midlands would be the ideal areas to keep Mary safe; it was a good distance from the borders and also from the English court in London. Elizabeth also had to consider the impact on her cousin, and other potential heir, Margaret Douglas; she and her husband were adamant that Mary was implicated in the death of their son. They were incandescent with rage that suggestions had been made to bring Mary to court; thankfully, Elizabeth was of a similar mind and that was never an option. Elizabeth's ego would never have allowed two queens to reside at her court; she had also heard of Mary's famed beauty and after her own bout of smallpox, which had left her marks on her skin, Elizabeth was not going to place herself beside her cousin.

The issue of Darnley's murder had to be settled if Mary was ever going to receive English support to regain her throne. In 1568, an inquiry was to be held in York and subsequently Westminster to ascertain if Mary was guilty of her husband's murder, but she refused from the outset to accept any verdict this inquiry would bring. In her mind, she was an anointed monarch and therefore above the law of any court that could try her; God, and God alone, was her judge so she refused to attend the inquiry at York and sent Lord Herries and the Bishop of Ross as her representatives instead.

Moray did attend the hearing and upon his arrival there presented the English lords with a casket which contained eight unsigned letters and love poems written in French, supposedly sent between Mary and Bothwell – these letters have subsequently become known as the Casket Letters. Moray explained the casket had been discovered in the keeping of one of Bothwell's servants following the defeat at Carberry Hill, and despite them being contained within a silver-gilt casket with the monogram of King Francois II on the top, Mary, who was not given the opportunity to examine them, denied she had written them and claimed them to be forgeries. The Duke of Norfolk sent the letters, which he described as horrible, to Elizabeth with the caveat that if these letters could be proved to be of Mary's hand, then they may condemn her as her husband's murderer.

The debate over the validity of these letters has raged for centuries. Many modern-day historians believe them to be fake or, at most, original letters written by Mary but with the incriminating passages inserted. Either that or they were letters written by Bothwell to someone else, or by Mary to someone else. Sadly, we will never know the truth as they were destroyed, probably by her son in order to protect his mother's reputation. The Scottish government had knowledge of the letters as early as December 1567 while Mary was a prisoner at Loch Levan, if they had been genuine would they not have produced them to the public as a clear sign of her guilt and as justification for their actions against her? Instead, they remained a secret until the inquiry of 1568 in York where they were studied in depth and where handwriting comparisons were made by the commissioners hired to ascertain her guilt.

The inquiry in York reached a stalemate so moved to London on the insistence of Elizabeth, who wanted the matter dealt with swiftly; the closeness to London meant time could be saved as no more travel would be needed from the court in London to the north. The Duke of Norfolk opened proceedings on 25 November. Moray once again produced the casket of letters at a hearing on 7 December and on 10 December he, along with other Scottish dignitaries, signed a deed that confirmed the letters had been written in Mary's own hand and had in no way been tampered with. On 14 December, a further meeting was held at Hampton Court at which members of the Privy Council compared other examples of Mary's known handwriting to the letters. Just as had happened in York a verdict of not proven was reached; the English councillors believed the letters to be genuine but Elizabeth did not want to openly accuse or deny Mary's guilt without concrete evidence against her so had little option but to declare an open verdict. The passing of this verdict protected Elizabeth from having to come face to face with Mary and also justified keeping her prisoner. Elizabeth was not willing to declare a fellow anointed queen a murderer, so Moray returned to Scotland and Mary remained a prisoner in England.

This left Elizabeth with a problem because if Mary was neither guilty nor innocent, should she not be afforded her freedom? Moray and his fellow lords who stood accused of imprisoning Mary had been allowed to leave and return to Scotland and he even retained his position as it's regent but Mary was to remain in custody, if neither was guilty then surely both must have been given their liberty. The ever-paranoid Elizabeth was never going to allow Mary her freedom, especially in England. It was not feasible for Mary to return to Scotland and there was no place for her at the English court; she was too much of a Catholic figurehead to have her freedom in England and so Mary had succeeded only in swapping her Scottish prison for an English one.

On 26 January 1569, Mary was moved again, this time she was placed under the supervision of Geroge Talbot, Earl of Shrewsbury, and his wife, the formidable Bess of Hardwick, at their home of Tutbury Castle in Staffordshire. It was a canny move to place her in the care of Shrewsbury, given that his properties were based in the Midlands, equidistance between England and Scotland and miles away from the coast, making any escape near enough impossible. Over the next few years, she was moved between the Shrewsbury residences at Sheffield Castle, Wingfield Manor and Chatsworth House. Despite her status as a prisoner, Mary was afforded certain luxuries. She had her own household, including a personal chef who prepared her many dishes which were served on the finest silver plate. Her rooms were richly decorated in fine tapestries and her bed made up with the finest linen. She was allowed a fair amount of time out of doors and was free to walk in grounds, under close supervision of course, and took the waters at nearby Buxton. Despite having a relatively comfortable imprisonment, Mary's health began to suffer and she soon developed rheumatism in her arms and legs, making it difficult for her to get around. She spent many an hour at her embroidery and no doubt brooding over the loss of her crown and her son.

In May 1569, Elizabeth attempted to negotiate a way back for her Scottish counterpart. The proposed deal was that Mary had to guarantee the Protestant faith and to ensure her people could openly practice that faith without censure or retribution. Unfortunately, the Scottish government were not interested in having Mary back as sovereign; she had caused nothing but issues and political instability and they had a young boy on the throne who they could manipulate and bend to their will.

In January 1570, the Earl of Moray was unexpectedly assassinated by James Hamilton, a Catholic supporter of Mary's. He managed to get a shot away even though Moray was at arms with nearly 150 men at his side. When Elizabeth heard the news of his death she was said to be devastated and shut herself away for hours in grief. The pair had formed a respectful and friendly working relationship and with his death Scotland once again became unstable and leaderless. Moray's death came shortly after a group of northern Catholic nobles attempted to rebel against Elizabeth and put Mary on the English throne. Known as the Northern Rebellion this was a genuine attempt to overthrow Elizabeth in favour of Mary. Based in Durham, it was led by Charles Neville, 6th Earl of Westmoreland, and Thomas Percy, 7th Earl of Northumberland. In retaliation Elizabeth ordered the Earl of Essex to raise an army to face the rebel forces. Essex's numbers reached over 10,000 while the rebels raised only 6,000 and when the rebels realised they were going to be vastly outnumbered, they abandoned plans to take York and instead turned back north to Barnard Castle. Realising there was little support for their plot, they abandoned the cause and fled over the border into Scotland. This act of rebellion raised the English court's suspicion of their illustrious prisoner even further, and caused the Scottish queen to be watched ever more closely with spies being placed among her household.

But it was not the end of the plotting. In 1571, Cecil discovered the Ridolfi plot. This was a Spanish-led plot to replace Elizabeth with Mary, it had been suggested the Duke of Norfolk marry Mary and return the country to Catholicism; the duke was later executed for his role in the plot. Mary was becoming a thorn in Elizabeth's side and the Parliament introduced a Bill that prevented Mary from ever taking the English throne – Elizabeth however, refused to give this royal assent. Proof perhaps that she still seriously considered Mary her heir; despite being her gaoler, perhaps Elizabeth wanted to keep Mary safe and out of harm's way so she could one day take the throne. But Elizabeth could never fully control the actions of her cousin and Mary was forever at the mercy of fantasy. From her fantastical upbringing in France to her passion-filled marriages, Mary Stewart had never really lived in reality and she was always one step away from her next misfortune.

Mary was never far from the centre of a number of plots surrounding her, but whether she was aware of them or not they proved disastrous for her. Following a further plot in 1583, Francis Walsingham introduced the Act for the Queen's Safety, otherwise known as the Act of Association, meaning that anyone caught plotting against the English monarch faced death. In 1584, sixteen years into her incarceration, Mary suggested she could return to Scotland and form an association with her son, James VI, which would see them rule jointly. This was another idea that made it no further than initial discussions, James was not far from his full majority so the prospect of sharing his throne with a mother he did not know seemed far-fetched to say the least. Mary had to accept that she was destined to remain in England as Elizabeth's captive queen.

Discovery of the Babington Plot in 1586 marked the beginning of the end for Mary – she was implicated in a plan to murder Elizabeth. A letter was discovered in which Mary gave her consent to the assassination of the English queen. Walsingham had infiltrated the plan by using double agents and had organised for one to place a secret message between the conspirators and Mary within the cork of a beer barrel, which was then intercepted and sent to Walsingham. As a result, Mary was arrested and put on trial at Fotheringhay Castle. She was tried for treason under the Act for the Queen's Safety; thirty-six noblemen, including her long-term gaoler the Earl of Shrewsbury, sat in judgement against her; on 25 October she was found guilty and sentenced to death. Elizabeth dithered over signing Mary's death warrant even when she faced pressure from her council; she could not reconcile herself to execute another queen, it was an act of regicide and that did not sit well with Elizabeth. Mary was also of Elizabeth's blood, one was a granddaughter and the other a great-granddaughter of Henry VII meaning they both had Tudor blood in their veins. Authorising the death would have been an agonising decision.

Elizabeth finally capitulated and signed the warrant on 1 February 1587. Mary was told on the evening of the 7th that she was to die the next morning. She spent her final hours in prayer with her ladies, she wrote her will and a letter to the King of France, Henri IV. The next morning Mary, Queen of Scots, at the age of 44 years old, climbed the three steps up to the scaffold which had been erected in the great hall at Fotheringhay. It had been draped in black cloth and on the floor lay a cushion for the queen to kneel on as she placed her head on the executioner's block. When she had forgiven the executioner, her ladies Jane Kennedy and Elizabeth Curle, helped remove their queen's outer clothing, as they did they revealed the Catholic queen was wearing a red gown, red being the colour of martyrdom, with a black bodice. She was then blindfolded and knelt on the cushion, she placed her neck on the block and stretched out her arms. Her final words were 'Into thy hands, O Lord, I commend my spirit'. Mary's head was not taken off with one blow, the first strike hit the back of her head, the second severed the neck, save a bit of sinew which was sliced through with the axe. Reports from her execution state that her lips moved for a time after her head was removed and that a small dog ran out from under her skirts. There are other accounts that do not include these details so they should be taken with a pinch of salt, but they do add to the romantic yet tragic life of Mary, Queen of Scots.

When news of Mary's death reached Elizabeth, she stated the Privy Council had acted without her consent. Apparently she had explicitly stated that the warrant was not to be acted upon; she did not want Mary's blood on her hands, but it was too late. Elizabeth denied

Mary's wish to buried in France, instead she ordered her to be buried at Peterborough Cathedral following a Protestant service, although her son James would later move her to Westminster Abbey where she lays to this day in a grand marble tomb.

With Mary now dead the number of heirs available to Elizabeth dwindled even further.

King James VI of Scotland

The death of his mother brought King James VI of Scotland one step closer to the English throne. If Elizabeth had abided by the wishes of her father Henry VIII, then James should not have been considered as her heir because for reasons unknown he had excluded the Scottish line of his elder sister Margaret Tudor, who had married James IV in 1503, in favour of his younger sister Mary. By this time the Grey sisters were dead but there was still the valid claim of Margaret Clifford, daughter of Eleanor Brandon and James's cousin, Arbella. Yet by the time Elizabeth died in 1603, Anne Clifford, daughter of Ferdinando Stanley, had succeeded to her grandmother Margaret Clifford's claim. There is no denying that Arbella, Anne and James had sound legitimate claims and despite James coming from the Scottish line he did stand closer to it in terms of his familial links. He and Arbella were first cousins and the great-great-grandchildren of Henry VII and his wife Elizabeth of York, while Lady Anne was their great-great-great-granddaughter. But because James's mother had also been a queen and he had descended from a line of great Scottish kings, he was by far the favourite choice. Having been crowned king of Scotland from a very young age, he also had also experience of ruling. The most crucial element in James's favour was the fact that he was a man and therefore could rule as a king, something England had not seen since 1537 when King Edward VI ascended the throne.

Born on 19 June 1566 at Edinburgh Castle James Charles Stuart was the son and only child of Mary, Queen of Scots, and her errant husband Henry Stuart, Lord Darnley. He was baptised in the December of 1566 at Stirling Castle and standing as his godparents were Charles IX of France (by proxy, John, Count of Brienne), Queen Elizabeth I of England (represented by Francis Russell, Earl of Bedford) and Emmanual Philibert, Duke of Savoy (represented by his Ambassador Philibert du Croc). One notable absence from the ceremony and celebrations afterward was James's father Darnley, as he was in dispute with his wife over a number of issues. The celebrations afterwards were held in the castle's great hall and lasted about three days. During that time gifts were exchanged, much food and drink was consumed with plenty of music played to be danced to. But what of James's father? Darnley was at the castle but refused to don his cloth of gold suit and join the celebrations as he was well aware what the foreign ambassadors thought of him – some refused to speak with him. Darnley had even joined in with the rumours that James was in fact the son of Mary's Italian secretary David Rizzio, who had been murdered just months earlier.

The baby Prince James was placed into the care of John Erskine, Earl of Mar, at Stirling Castle, times were troubled for Mary and the safety of a fortress castle like Stirling would ensure her son and heir would remain unharmed. As like many countries across Europe at the time, Scotland was in the midst of religious upheaval, which made it unstable and a tempestuous place to be. The queen was a committed Catholic but the Protestant faction, calling themselves the Lords of the Congregation, stood in direct opposition to her. Mary tried her best to strike a balance between the Catholics and the Protestants but that could only go so far, something would have to give and that came when she decided to baptise her son in the Catholic faith. The kirk wanted Mary to relent and have James baptised in to the Protestant faith but she refused, which resulted in the queen openly going against the wishes of the Scottish kirk, something that was not acceptable among the high-ranking nobles or those who fully supported Scotland's newly reformed Kirk. It was not just the fact that she was a Catholic, but the fact she had envisioned a Catholic future for Scotland by having the future king baptised in the Catholic faith. It left her lords with no option, it meant she had to be removed from her throne before James became to indoctrinated by Rome.

Following the baptism Darnley fled to his father's estates in Glasgow, he was concerned that the men who had plotted to kill Rizzio were seeking revenge after he had divulged their names to Mary. But it was not their plotting that Mary was concerned about, it was his. She decided to entice him back to Edinburgh where she could keep a closer eye on him. The fatal explosion at Kirk o' Field shocked many but the fact that Mary recklessly married the chief suspect so soon after can be endlessly speculated over. The queen claimed James Hepburn, the Earl of Bothwell, had kidnapped and raped her, leaving her reputation in tatters and with no option but to marry him. Bothwell was a Protestant; he had even refused to enter the chapel to witness the baptism of James and yet here she was marrying him in a Protestant service at Holyrood. Had he bewitched the queen so much that she was willing to turn a blind eye to his religion, and his crimes? James now had a Protestant stepfather who, along with his mother, stood accused of murdering his father. Mary had fallen pregnant by Bothwell and when the pair faced the rebels at Carberry Hill in June 1567 she refused to let Bothwell suffer, instead she gave herself up in order to secure him a safe passage out of the country. In turn she was imprisoned and forced to abdicate her throne in favour of the 1-year-old James.

This turn of events brought Mary's half-brother James Stewart, Earl of Moray, in to the role of regent, and one of the first things he did was have the young James crowned king. The ceremony took place at Stirling Castle on 29 July 1567, it was a sparsely attended ceremony, but by having James crowned and Moray as regent meant the Protestant faction had at last gained control of Scotland. As we are aware, Mary managed to escape her imprisonment from Loch Levan and made her way into England in the hope that Elizabeth would aid her attempt to win back her throne. This was not forthcoming and all she faced was further imprisonment.

Thankfully, King James was far too young to fully understand what was happening around him and that his mother south of the border, stood accused of murdering his father. In time he would learn of her misdeeds, but that knowledge would come from Mary's enemies who purposely set about blackening her name across Scotland and Europe, referring to her as being wicked, a murderess a whore and a witch. The author of these slanders was George Buchanan, a well-respected historian and scholar. He was hired as James's tutor and through him James learned to hate his mother and to loathe her religion; it was nothing short of brainwashing. Because James was so young, like Elizabeth was when her mother Anne Boleyn was executed, he could have had no real memories of his mother. James remained in the custody of the Earl and Countess of Mar at Stirling Castle, and to James they were his parents; they protected him and saw to his welfare, but at the same time they made sure he had no positive views of either of his parents. To him they were to be feared as dangerous.

James remained at Stirling as he grew older, protected and away from any political strife that was engulfing the country. His education ramped up. He was taught to speak Latin and Greek from a young age, but struggled with mathematics – which may explain his lack of ability to keep track of his spending later on in life. But while James sat in the classroom in Stirling Castle, his mother did not sit quietly in England. Her viewpoint was that she had been forced to sign her abdication and it therefore was invalid; as far as she was concerned, she was Scotland's true and rightful monarch – sadly she was in the minority in thinking this. The Marian supporters had no leader and the chance of a restoration was slipping from her grasp. But that was not to say there was no plotting going on on her behalf. Moray was not a popular choice as regent; he was the illegitimate son of James V and was considered an inappropriate person to be making decisions in the name of the king. He had been given prior warning that he was not popular and that an attempt might be made on his life, but he chose to ignore those warnings and was assassinated in Linlithgow –

much to Mary's delight, which was a reflection of how fractured their relationship had become. When Mary had first returned to Scotland from France she relied heavily on her half-brother, but over time their religious differences and Mary's choices in husband caused a rift so big that she was pleased to hear of his death.

James was only 3 years old when his uncle was murdered so would have not remembered him through his own recollections, but must have been told about him from Mar; given that an older James later referred to him as a 'bastard rebel', we can only assume they taught him to dislike Moray too. Given his tender years, James and Scotland needed another regent, someone who could guide the country through troubled waters and who could prepare James for his life as king. That job fell to Matthew Stewart, 4th Earl of Lennox, husband of Margaret Douglas and father to Lord Darnley, making him James's paternal grandfather and the only family member the young king ever had around him. Lennox's appointment was greeted well in England; he had lived there for many years and decreed to rule Scotland in accordance with English policy, much to Elizabeth's delight. But for him, the most important thing was his grandson, he wanted to ensure James was safe and would inherit a country that was sound and stable when he reached his majority.

On 28 August 1571 at the age of 5, James made his long-awaited public debut with the state opening of parliament; sadly it was not to be the glittering affair that we expect today. James's ceremonial entrance into Stirling was mooted to say the least. The Honours of Scotland lay under Marian control in Edinburgh Castle so a sword and sceptre were made from wood and painted gold, which were then carried before the young monarch. James read out a prepared speech to those in attendance in it, the king officially appointed Lennox his regent and guardian. It had taken a long time for Lennox to return to Scotland and take up power and now he did so in the right of his grandson the king. Sadly, being the king's grandfather meant nothing and Mary's supporters were soon plotting his downfall.

On 3 September 1571 a gang of Hamilton supporters, the natural enemies of the Lennox family, raised Stirling against the regent, the Earl of Mar had managed to fight back but in the melee Lennox was fatally shot. He managed to return to the castle where the young king watched as his dying grandfather was carried into the great hall. Poor James had lost both parents and now had to witness the agonising death of the only family member he had ever known; he had liked his grandfather very much and would remember his death for the rest of his life, using it as a constant reminder of what violence can do. The Earl of Mar was now declared regent, a decision that pleased England and meant the young king felt some kind of continuity. But it was his tutors who had full control of the king's impressionable mind and could shape him to their will. George Buchanan was James's main tutor and although he was not necessarily anti-monarchy, he was definitely suspicious of the divine right of kings, a belief James would believe strongly in. Buchanan was against the glory of monarchy and all the trappings that go with a glittering court. He was adamant James should learn that he was just a young Scottish boy who happened to be king, a title that was given and taken by the will of the people, and one that did not place him above anyone. He must learn to be a good and godly person in the Protestant faith and if he should prove himself otherwise then he would be removed from his position, just like his mother.

There have been suggestions that Buchanan resorted to violence whenever James struggled to grasp his alternate ideas. The Countess of Mar chastised Buchanan when she found him striking the king on his backside, 'Madam, I have whipt his arse: you may kiss it if you please', was his terse response. Clearly the countess knew how to respect her monarch, regardless of his age. When James was old enough to understand, Buchanan took much delight in teaching him all about his devious and wicked mother, that she was the very embodiment of what was wrong with the monarchy and James should strive to be the opposite of her. Regent Mar died at the end of October 1572 and in his place came the Earl of Morton. There were suspicions surrounding Mar's death as it came shortly after he had dined with Morton. For James it meant a new guardian, but his daily life went on as it had before, dominated by Buchanan.

James was taught to ride and hunt, which would become one of the greatest loves of his life. He developed a bawdy sense of humour and often made those around him the butt of his jokes, knowing they had to just stand and take the supposedly funny insults thrown at them by the king; from a young age he understood his own importance. At the age of 11, James decided he was ready to rule his country alone, Regent Morton tendered his resignation, but some were not happy – mainly supporters of his mother Mary – and tried to seize Stirling Castle where a violent skirmish broke out. Later, in 1578, James finally announced he had come of age and was escorted to Edinburgh by 3,000 men on horseback. James needed guidance and Esme Stewart, Earl of Lennox (later the Duke) arrived at the Scottish court from France. Lennox was a kinsman of the king and the two formed a strong friendship, though he was not well liked for his influence over the king; when he had Morton beheaded in 1581, alarm bells started to ring. In England, Elizabeth was worried Lennox would reignite the Auld Alliance between Scotland and France, but the biggest fear was that he would persuade James to bring back his mother. Those against Lennox knew the only way to separate him from James was to kidnap the king. A group of nobles managed to lure James to a deer hunt near Ruthven Castle, from there they took him into their custody on 23 August 1582 and held him there for nearly a year. During that time Lennox was ordered to leave Scotland, which he did in June 1583.

With Lennox gone, James was freed and immediately took control of the Kirk, becoming the head of the Church of Scotland; he also ordered any copies of Buchanan's work that vilified his mother to be destroyed. Sadly, James did not enjoy his freedom for long. He was captured once again by a group of lords and forced to accept their terms. In 1586 the king signed a treaty with Elizabeth which brought peace and a pension of £4,000 per annum. Elizbeth also agreed not to hinder his claim to her throne, was this an early indication that James was Elizabeth's preferred choice?

The relationship between James and Elizabeth was complex at best, he tried to please her but she showed very little interest in him. He referred to her as his sister and sometimes his mother, which given she was his godmother does not seem that strange. Despite both being monarchs in their own realms, James never appears to have challenged or questioned Elizabeth, she seems to have been a dominant force and someone James could look up to and respect. But when his mother was caught up in a Catholic plot to remove Elizabeth from her throne, James pleaded with the English queen to spare his mother's life. His pleas went unheard and his mother was executed on Elizabeth's orders. The details of her execution were relayed to James and from that point he was unable to ever discuss the details of his mother's death again. Did he feel guilt that he had not done more to help her? Perhaps. But in reality he was in no position to help her, especially in the early days when he was still young and dominated by others.

By 1589, James was 23 and his language had become coarse and bawdy; the time came for him to find a bride so and he looked to Denmark and the daughter of Frederick II, the Princess Anna. They seemed smitten from the off, they shared love notes and plans were quickly put in place for Anna to sail to Scotland. Unfortunately the weather was against her and her fleet was forced back to the coast of Norway where she sought refuge in Oslo until it was safe to sail. James heard the news of the great storm and worried for the safety of his bride. He kept watch on the Firth of Forth and ordered prayers to be said for the safe delivery of the future queen. What James did not know in mid-September was that Anna was safe in Oslo after trying at least five times to set sail. By October Anna had managed to write to James to tell him she was safe in Oslo and would remain there for the winter. Determined to claim his bride, James set sail from Leith with a retinue of around 300 arriving in Oslo on 19 November where upon meeting Anna for the first time kissed her on the lips, as was the Scottish custom. King James and Princess Anna were officially married on 23 November 1589 at the Old Bishop's Palace in Oslo. They spent time in Norway before James made the visit to his new family at Kronborg Castle, Elsinore, Denmark. The newlyweds were met by Anna's mother Queen Sophie, and her 12-year-old brother King Christian IV. From there they travelled to Copenhagen to attend the wedding of Anna's sister, and on 21 April 1590, the king and queen finally set sail for Scotland, arriving at Leith on 1 May. Anna was crowned queen on 17 May at Holyrood in what was the first Protestant coronation in Scottish history.

Life in Scotland was becoming increasingly unstable at this point and there was one murderous plot after another – nobles were murdering each other and there was even a plot to kill the king himself. Holyrood came under direct attack in 1591 leaving James and Anna stricken and having to be rescued. In 1593 Falkland Palace in Fife came under siege, forcing the king and queen to take refuge in the tower. By 1600 life seemed steadier once more. Anna and James had three surviving children, he had control over the kirk and life was peaceful in Scotland for the first time in years. In 1603 James's life, and the lives of his family and countrymen, was about to change forever as the death of Queen Elizabeth brought him to the English throne.

Chapter Five

King James I of England and the Birth of the Stuart Dynasty

The Death of Queen Elizabeth I

The first few weeks of 1601 were particularly tough on the queen. Her one-time favourite Robert Deveraux, Earl of Essex, was arrested following a planned attack to force his way into Elizabeth's presence. Essex had been opposed to James's succession, so following his execution on a charge of treason, Robert Cecil was free to open secret lines of communication with King James in Scotland. Cecil was the main instigator behind James becoming the next king of England and he assured the Scottish king that if he followed his guidance, when the time came the crown would be his. Naturally, James was happy to oblige, but Elizabeth still refused to officially name her heir – in fact she vehemently refused to talk about the succession with anyone. This angered James, he saw no reason why she could not openly name him; he was her preferred choice and her reluctance to publicly acknowledge that brought tension to their relationship.

The execution of Essex lay heavy on Elizabeth's mind and she became tearful and suffered bouts of depression. State business began to suffer as the queen preferred to isolate herself from her court, she told the French ambassador that 'She was tired of life, for nothing now contented her or gave her any enjoyment.' Her popularity had begun to wane and her court was becoming tired and weary, her courtiers were looking to the one who would succeed her, in the hope of reassurance and of getting one step ahead of their rivals. Groups of courtiers had their own candidate for the succession and they would want to be in favour when the time came.

In 1601, England was in a sorry state. Costly wars against Spain and Ireland came with little return and had left the exchequer empty. Crops were failing due to drought and many people were starving as a result. The irony was that if Elizabeth's father Henry VIII had not dissolved the monasteries the poor would have had somewhere to turn for refuge. Now, they had little choice but to flood the streets and beg for what they could. As the country failed, so did its queen. But in the summer of 1602 Elizabeth managed to rally enough strength to enjoy a summer progress and wet weather returned, meaning the harvest flourished and the famine came to an end. As Christmas drew closer, however, it was clear to all that Elizabeth's health was deteriorating. She once again fell into a deep depression and refused all food; she made her last public appearance on 6 February 1603, when she received a Venetian named Giovanni Scarameli. She sat regally on a dais in a sumptuous low-cut gown of silver and white taffeta embroidered with gold, she wore strings of pearls and rubies round her neck, and on her head, a crown.

The Catholic Doge of Venice had always seen Elizabeth as a usurper and a heretic, unworthy of his acknowledgment. But now the Venetians needed her cooperation. Piracy was rife and it was the English who led the way in hauling loot from the Venetians' ships to their own. Scarameli had been sent by the Doge to plead with Elizabeth to call off her men. Scarameli lowered himself and kissed the hem of her dress, she raised him up so he could kiss her hand. She then rebuffed the poor Venetian, who took the brunt of her anger at never having been acknowledged as queen and never receiving a visit to her court in the near forty-five years of her reign.

On the last day of January in 1603 Elizabeth left Whitehall for the sumptuous surroundings of Richmond Palace, a luxurious Thameside Palace built by her grandfather Henry VII in 1501 following a devastating fire at Sheen Palace. In the middle of February, Elizabeth suffered a huge loss when her friend and kinswoman Katherine Carey, the Countess of Nottingham, died at Richmond. Katherine Carey was the daughter of Henry Carey, 1st Baron Hunsdon, the son of William Carey and Mary Boleyn, Elizabeth's aunt. Katherine had married Charles Howard, Earl of Nottingham, in July 1563 and the marriage produced five children. Even though she was a dedicated wife and mother Katherine, who was appointed First Lady of the Bedchamber, had been at Elizabeth's side from the moment she became queen and this loyalty was returned as she sat at the deathbed of her dearest and oldest friend. Katherine was rewarded for her service with a state funeral as ordered by the queen.

This death plunged Elizabeth further in to an ever darker depression, from which she never really recovered. Around this time the queen's coronation ring had to be cut loose from her finger. It had become embedded in her finger causing the surrounding flesh to become inflamed and painful. The symbolism of Elizabeth's marriage to her nation coming to an end was not lost on anyone and she must have felt her own death was near. She began to suffer with a pain in her throat which was possibly caused by ulcers or an abscess, making it difficult for her to swallow and by the beginning of March she was suffering from a fever. This then led to an insatiable thirst and pains in her stomach. Looked at in isolation, none of these symptoms were a huge cause for concern, but looked at collectively, and with her depressive state, they were a huge worry. It was clear the queen was dying, so Cecil informed Robert Carey, a kinsman of the queen, to be ready to ride to Scotland with the news and to announce to James that he was now King of England; in readiness he had horses placed at staging posts going north.

Elizabeth was now laid on the floor on a pile of cushions; her mouth was dry, she could not eat, drink or sleep, and had stayed in the same clothes for nearly three weeks. People pleaded with her to return to her bed but she was too weak to move and refused. It was not until 21 March that she was finally persuaded to retire to her bed. The abscess in her throat burst which brough some relief, but it was only a temporary respite and soon she was unable to talk at all. She laid on her side and had no communication with anyone except the Archbishop of Canterbury, John Whitgift, and her chaplains.

Given Elizabeth's state of ill health it is surprising that she still did not name her heir. Her argument had always been that she did not want the heir to become a focal point for a rebellion against her, but as she became increasingly ill at the beginning of 1603 there was no danger of her being ousted from the throne. Her reluctance must have been rooted in other meanings too, did she struggle to accept there would be another monarch after her? Did she feel an element of guilt of never marrying and having her own Tudor heir? As she lay on her deathbed, Cecil asked again for her to name her successor but by now it was too late as she was unable to talk; rumour has it that she made a gesture – whether that be a nod of the head or the sign of a crown – that James was her choice. In order for James to become the hereditary ruler of England Elizabeth needed to name him verbally, otherwise he would be seen as the elected ruler and with that came the possibility of removal at a later date. Whether Elizabeth managed this is debatable. James did not like the idea of being an elected ruler, he had Tudor blood in his veins via his great-grandmother, Margaret Tudor, and so felt he was well deserved of the English throne through dynastic rights.

Elizabeth, Queen of England, died in the early hours of 24 March 1603 and with her death came the end of the Tudor dynasty and England's Glorious Age. Lady Scrope removed a sapphire ring from Elizabeth's finger and dropped it from a window to an already mounted Robert Carey below. He set off for Scotland, determined to reach Edinburgh before anyone else. That same morning, King James VI of Scotland was proclaimed King James I of England. The news was met by a subdued crowd who were mourning the loss of their queen who had ruled for nearly forty-five years. By the evening, however, the bonfires were lit and the bells were tolling as the dawn of a new era began.

At midnight on 26 March 1603 Robert Carey arrived at Holyrood, after galloping for three days straight from London. The king was roused immediately and Carey handed to him the blue sapphire ring that told the Scottish king Elizabeth was dead and he was now king of England. Robert Carey being the first person to greet him as thus.

Elizabeth's body lay at Richmond before being conveyed by barge down the Thames to Whitehall Palace to lie in state. From Whitehall Elizabeth made her last journey to Westminster Abbey on 28 April 1603, where her funeral was attended by thousands of people. Her coffin was draped in rich purple velvet and was drawn by on a bier by four great grey horses draped in black, atop her coffin lay a funeral effigy. James would later erect a white marble tomb in remembrance of her with the inscription:

> Sacred to memory: Religion to its primitive purity restored, peace settled, money restored to its just value, domestic rebellion quelled, France relieved when involved with intestine divisions; the Netherlands supported; the Spanish Armada vanquished; Ireland almost lost by rebels, eased by routing the Spaniard; the revenues of both universities much enlarged by a Law of Provisions; and lastly, all England enriched. Elizabeth, a most prudent governor 45 years, a victorious and triumphant Queen, most strictly religious, most happy, by a calm and resigned death at her 70th year left her mortal remains, till by Christ's Word they shall rise to immortality, to be deposited in the Church [the Abbey], by her established and lastly founded. She died the 24th of March, Anno 1602 [this is Old Style dating, now called 1603], of her reign the 45th year, of her age the 70th.
>
> To the eternal memory of Elizabeth queen of England, France and Ireland, daughter of King Henry VIII, grand-daughter of King Henry VII, great-grand-daughter to King Edward IV. Mother of her country, a nursing-mother to religion and all liberal sciences, skilled in many languages, adorned with excellent endowments

> both of body and mind, and excellent for princely virtues beyond her sex. James, king of Great Britain, France and Ireland, hath devoutly and justly erected this monument to her whose virtues and kingdoms he inherits.

King James Heads to England

James did not waste time in making preparations for his journey south. He bade farewell to the people of Edinburgh and turned south towards England, Anna and his children were to follow later. James was met at Berwick by Sir John Carey, brother of Sir Robert, and was handed the ceremonial keys to the castle which he immediately handed back, the significance being that the responsibility of the castle and people to defend their town was entrusted by the king. Berwick was the gateway to England from the north and had long been fought over by the Scots and English in border skirmishes. The reasons for Anna's delayed journey have been debated; one explanation is that trouble was expected as James travelled through the northern parts of England and he didn't want to expose his wife and children to risk. The over reason was that Anna's new retinue of English women would not be prepared to receive her as they were still in mourning for Elizabeth; either way, Queen Anna, the heir Prince Henry and the Princess Elizabeth, were to remain in Scotland until the summons came. The regal progress to England was not going to be cheap and the new clothes, horses and coaches were paid for by the people of Edinburgh, which was very much resented by the Scottish government who objected to Scottish money going into England; they were soon pacified when James subsequently used the English coffers to reward his loyal Scottish men with gifts and pensions, which caused huge upset and anger among the English.

James first step on English soil came at the border town of Berwick, where he was greeted by Sir John Carey. The cannons fired from the castle in welcome and when James was handed the keys to the castle, he promptly knighted the porter and handed them straight back, as was the custom. The town square was full of dignitaries, the mayor greeted his new king and handed him a purse full of gold coins; James made his way to the church were a service was led by the Bishop of Durham. In the evening bonfires were lit and the town rejoiced in the coming of their king. The following morning the English convoy arrived to greet James and escort him down through Northumberland, where he was lavishly entertained.

The journey south was eventful; the crowds were large and shouted 'God Save King James!' He was showered with lavish gifts as he entered each town and was invited to hunt the vast forests. At York the king lodged at the King's Manor and walked through the streets to the Minster where a service of thanksgiving was heard. The wine flowed through the streets and entertainments were laid on. Word spread that the king liked to hunt and enjoy the spoils so there were plenty of feasts of wild game waiting for him. It was while lodged in York that he was met by Robert Cecil, Secretary of State, the man responsible for putting him on the English throne. James confirmed Cecil in his post, knowing he had the best political mind in England; he would be grateful to Cecil and his advice, as he knew very little about his new country. From York the growing royal progress made its way south to Doncaster and then through to Burghley House in Lincolnshire, and beyond to Rutland. King James arrived at Theobalds on the 3 May, a place he would come to love and eventually own. It was a grand red-brick three storey building set in magnificent grounds and far more extravagant than James had ever seen in Scotland. Throughout his journey he knighted 906 men and bestowed royal favour on many more, and by the time he reached London people were clamouring to see their new king.

Thee government of Scotland had to continue as James journeyed south to claim his new throne, so he left the Earls of Dunfermline and Mar as heads of the Privy Council. In Westminster he retained many of Elizabeth's administration and added a handful of his Scottish lords for good measure. He was generous with his mainly Scottish household – but had to be told numerous times that the money pit was not bottomless. England was far richer than Scotland, but it too had its limits. The country was at war with Spain and the Irish were on the brink of rebellion, the county's finances were not in great shape, with expenses far outweighing revenue. To ease the financial burden James made peace with Spain and came to an agreement with the Irish – if they were willing to accept him as king then he would be happy to draw a line under the rebellion and offer pardons to those involved. James knew war was expensive and, just like he had done previously in Scotland, he knew making peace would save money. It was not just war that cost money; James's household expenditure was excessive and far outweighed Elizabeth's – but then he was married with three children to support, so naturally he would require extra funds. The problem was both he and Anna were fond of fine jewels and luxury clothes, making his money problems worse. When he entertained, he made sure he did it well. Alcohol flowed freely, which led to problems with the king's behaviour and often his feasts ended in riotous behaviour.

James was a lover of architecture and commissioned the architect Inigo Jones to design a new banqueting house at Whitehall Palace. Both James and Anna enjoyed masques and wanted to create a purpose-built place for them to entertain. The banqueting house was completed in 1622 and today is the only survivor of the fire of 1698, which burned the rest of the palace to the ground.

It did not take long for the anti-Scottish resentment to build amongst the English. They did not like to see their money lining the pockets of Scottish noblemen who were now in the most prominent roles at court, including Gentleman of the Bedchamber. It would seem James was surrounding himself with Scots in a bid to keep the English at bay, but this was England and an English court, and so the English nobles were willing to make their views known. Feathers were ruffled by the amount of time James spent hunting; he needed to focus on kingly duties in his new realm rather than on the hunt. James's solution to this was to take his secretaries hunting with him so he could work if the need arose.

On 11 June 1603 Queen Anna made her journey with her two eldest children, leaving the young and sickly Prince Charles in Scotland as he was thought too weak to make the long journey. Anna and the children showed James as being a dedicated family man, and for the first time in many years England had a royal family with young children. Prince Henry, the newly created Prince of Wales, was athletic, healthy and well-liked, while the Princess Elizabeth was the jewel in James's crown and would prove to be a valuable asset for England in the political marriage market. Disaster would strike when Henry died at the age of 18 after contracting typhoid fever in the lead up to the celebration of the marriage of his beloved sister Elizabeth. Henry's body was laid to rest at Westminster Abbey, not far from the tomb of his grandmother Mary, Queen of Scots. The death of Henry made Prince Charles the heir to the English throne. Thankfully, the ailments of his early childhood seemed to be behind him.

So, James VI of Scotland settled into life as James I of England and the Jacobean era began. While James had many flaws his people enjoyed peace and low taxes; when he died on 27 March 1625 at the age of 58 his people mourned his loss. He was a different kind of monarch to Elizabeth, she was the embodiment of what a true monarch should be, but times were changing. The old Tudor world had largely gone and in its place came James and his Stuart dynasty.

Chapter Six

Other Contenders

Charles Stuart, Earl of Lennox

For a brief moment it looked like England had a male heir to ascend the throne. A man that has for so often been overlooked in favour of his elder brother, Henry, Lord Darnley. But Charles was the complete opposite of his brother. While Darnley was tall, athletic and physically strong, Charles was weak and hated physical activities such as hunting and dancing. Darnley was well educated and well-read, whereas Charles is believed to have read just two books in his life, Aristotle and the Book of Common Prayer. Despite being fluent in French, Charles is said to have been a slow learner and may even have suffered with some kind of learning difficulties. But Charles's childhood was far from conventional.

He was born sometime between April and May in 1557 at Temple Newsam, Yorkshire. The fact he was born in England gave him a slight advantage over his nephew James, who as a Scot would have been considered a foreigner and therefore unable to claim the throne. With so much attention and focus being put into Darnley's upbringing Charles seemed almost like an afterthought for his parents. Margaret and Matthew, the Countess and Earl of Lennox, had seen six of their children die shortly after birth or in early infancy, so when Darnley survived and began to grow into a strong and healthy young man all their attention turned to his advancement. He was given the best tutors, was dressed in the finest clothes and taught that he was important and could expect grand things. He was a man destined to be a king and that is what his parents prepared him for. All the while Charles, who was roughly about eleven years younger than Darnley, watched as his brother became King Consort of Scotland and was then later brutally murdered.

When his parents were taken prisoner in London, Charles was left up in Yorkshire at the family home at Settrington. He was about 8 years old and was forced to be separated from his family yet again when he was placed in the care of the Archbishop of York. He was kept under close surveillance as there were concerns that he might try to leave. Darnley had gone missing, presumably he had escaped to the Continent, and the last thing England needed was another Catholic male with Tudor blood to go missing. Settrington lay just thirty miles from the Yorkshire coast and an ambush was possible. Once Darnley and Lennox were dead, Margaret found herself with just one child left to her; Charles was important all of a sudden – he was a potential heir to Elizabeth I and his marriage would be of importance. As we already know, Margaret Douglas was ruthless when it came to the dynastic progression of her children and was not afraid to break rules to get what she wanted.

Margaret Douglas, Countess of Lennox, and Bess of Hardwick, Countess of Shrewsbury, were two of the country's leading ladies, and while Bess was a close friend of the queen's, Margaret was not. Despite being cousins Margaret and Elizabeth did not get along, Margaret was born of a true queen whereas Elizabeth, she deemed, was not. Bess's daughter, Elizabeth Cavendish, was of marriageable age and when she learned that her good friend was looking for a bride for her son, they secretly opened negotiations. Both knew that Elizabeth would decline the marriage proposal so they decided to engineer it for themselves, which was a risky game to play. The plan was that Margaret and Charles would travel north, supposedly on their way to Scotland; Elizabeth agreed to this on one condition, they must not visit Mary, Queen of Scots, enroute. It just so happened that Mary was being held by Bess's husband, George Talbot, Earl of Shrewsbury, but Margaret promised her queen she would not visit her former daughter-in-law. Bess must have viewed the marriage with Charles as an ideal opportunity to advance her daughter far beyond any role she could have dreamed of. Was Bess hoping to persuade Elizabeth to name Charles her heir, thereby make her daughter a queen? From Margaret's point of view, she was desperate for money so this was a purely financial deal, if the couple fell in love, then their happiness would be a fortunate by-product. Following the death of her son and husband Margaret had lost vast estates and was almost destitute, whereas the Shrewsburys were incredibly wealthy and with Elizabeth's dowry Margaret could ease some of her financial burden. Unknown to her, Bess's husband was not happy with the plan and refused to put forward any money.

The two countesses engineered a chance meeting and the young couple fell for each other immediately. They were married at Rufford Abbey and it looked like a match made in heaven, but once again royal authority was not gained prior to the marriage and, given Charles's close proximity to the throne, they must have expected Elizabeth's wrath to come down on them all. It was the Earl of Shrewsbury who confessed the secret marriage to the queen, he was angry that it had gone ahead after he had expressed his doubts. Elizabeth was apoplectic with rage and Margaret, Charles and his new bride Elizabeth, were summoned back to London. Bess was ordered to stay where she was and it looked like she was going to dodge any serious punishment; Bess and her husband had done huge favours for the crown by keeping Queen Mary in their care. It was clear that Elizabeth was going to place all the blame on her cousin.

Margaret, Charles and Elizabeth arrived in Hackney mid-December and went to Margaret's residence, Kings Place, a house formerly owned by her beloved uncle Henry VIII. The day after their arrival home Margaret was summoned to court where she learned a full investigation was to be carried out. The queen was convinced there was a plot to remove her and replace her with either Charles or with Queen Mary. But, as promised, Margaret declared she had not once seen, or had any communication with, the former Scottish queen or with Bess; these details were backed up and verified by members of her household. It appeared the marriage had happened purely by chance; Elizabeth was satisfied but ordered them all to stay under house arrest in Hackney. I'd say they got off lightly considering her treatment of Katherine Grey, maybe the queen secretly favoured this match. The young Elizabeth was pregnant with her and Charles's first child; if that baby was a boy, then he ticked every box to make him a future king of England.

On 18 April 1572 James VI of Scotland conferred the title Earl of Lennox on his uncle Charles, a move which pleased queen Elizabeth. Sadly, he did not enjoy good health and died of consumption just eighteen months after his marriage to Elizabeth – just a few short months after the birth of his daughter, Arbella. Charles Stuart had had a very strong claim on the English throne, but as another potential claimant passed away so a new one emerged; Charles's claim was passed to his young daughter, first cousin to James VI, Lady Arbella Stuart.

Lady Arbella Stuart

The details surrounding Arbella's birth are scant to say the least. The first reference that we have is a letter dated 17 November 1575 written by Arbella's grandmother, Margaret Douglas, to Mary, Queen of Scots, from Hackney in which there is a mention of the infant. Given Arbella's elevated state you might be forgiven for assuming her birth was important enough to be recorded, but as with other ladies of rank, Lady Jane Grey for example, this was not always the case, especially with girls. Again, we have few details regarding her baptism but it would more than likely have taken place not long after her birth as was custom at the time, and would probably have taken place at the nearby church of St Augustine. We can only speculate as to her godparents, but it has been suggested that her uncle Charles Cavendish, her aunt Mary Cavendish and her husband

Gilbert Talbot, later the 7th Earl of Shrewsbury, fulfilled the roles, although this may be based on the relationship she had with them in adulthood.

Arbella's grandmothers were very influential during her younger years. Margaret was to fight for Arbella's right to the Lennox title and estates which had reverted back to the Scottish crown following the early death of her father, Charles. Margaret was deep in debt to the English crown due to her many fines and confiscation of land following her numerous times in the Tower, so she could little afford to lose Arbella's inheritance. Bess of Hardwick petitioned to her friend Elizabeth I to intervene on her granddaughter's behalf, but the Regent Morton argued that because she had been born outside of the realm of Scotland, Arbella had no right to the title.

Margaret Douglas died on 7 March 1578 when Arbella was not yet 3 years old, so any hope of gaining the Lennox land was all but gone. One thing she had hoped to pass to her granddaughter was a casket containing the Lennox jewels which Arbella was to receive at the age of 14. In the meantime, they were entrusted into the safe keeping of Thomas Fowler, the Executor of Margaret's estate. Sadly, Fowler absconded to Scotland with the jewels, which he passed straight to King James. Again, Bess pleaded with Elizabeth to intervene and recover the jewels but the queen refused, stating she had no jurisdiction in Scotland. Instead she awarded Arbella with a payment of £200 per year and her mother Elizabeth £400. Despite these payments they could no longer afford to rent the house in Hackney so Arbella left London with her mother and returned to Derbyshire. Elizabeth was not keen on this idea as Mary, Queen of Scots, was the prisoner of Bess's husband and it was thought she could be a bad influence on the young Arbella; so she was sent with her mother to live at Chatsworth, while the rest of the family were residing at Sheffield Castle. Following protests from Bess and Cecil, the queen soon relented .

At the age of 3 Arbella began her formal education. This may seem young to us but it was important to begin early as she could be married as young as 13. She was taught Latin and French, which would have been a desired as it would enable her to converse with foreign dignitaries should the need arise in her future. She would also have had a decent grasp of geography as well as the more feminine subjects such as embroidery, stitching and dancing. Hunting and riding were also important pursuits when it came to a noble-born lady who was looking for a husband.

Despite Elizabeth's wishes it was inevitable that Arbella would spend time in the company of her aunt, Mary, and by all accounts they got on very well. No doubt the young Arbella would have been in awe of the tall and beautiful Scottish queen whose life had been luxurious when she was the French queen, and no doubt Mary enthralled her niece with stories of the grand French court. What Arbella had to be reminded of was that for all Mary's grandeur, she was a prisoner who lived under supervision and had limitations on her freedom.

On 21 January 1582 Arbella's mother Elizabeth died at Sheffield Priory at the age of just 26. Prior to her death she wrote to the queen asking that she allow her mother, Bess, to take full legal custody of Arbella who was aged around 7 when her mother passed away. Bess had also been asked by her daughter to take care of Arbella until she was aged 16 or married, whichever event occurred first, at which point she was to receive the money Elizabeth had left for her daughter. Queen Elizabeth was left unmoved by Arbella's plight. Despite pleading letters reminding her that Arbella was her own blood kin, she callously took back the £400 that had been paid to her mother rather than pay it on to Arbella. This prompted Bess to remind Cecil and Elizabeth that £600 was not a suitable amount for the upkeep of someone so close to the throne. The queen did not relent.

Bess took the guardianship of her granddaughter very seriously. She taught her everything she would need to know about household management because when she married she would be expected to run her own estates. Arbella was a huge catch in the marriage market and any man willing to offer would have to adapt to perhaps one day being king beside his wife. There was talk of her marrying her cousin King James, a match which his captive mother approved of. A marriage with James would have made Arbella Queen of Scotland from a young age and strengthened both their claims to the English throne. But this idea went no further than just talk as James showed little interest in marrying his younger cousin. Next in line came Robert Dudley, Lord Denbigh, the young son of Robert Dudley, Earl of Leicester, and his second wife Lettice Knollys; Denbigh was aged just 4 to Arbella's 8 when talk of a match began in 1583. This talk however, infuriated the Scottish queen and caused a rift between herself and Bess. Mary felt that because Leicester was Elizabeth's favourite it would steer the English throne away from her son James and towards Arbella. Bess and Mary were now at war and the whole family was drawn into the mess created by the potential Shrewsbury marriage. Sadly, the young Robert Dudley died just a month after the negotiations began, but it did provide an opportunity for Queen Elizabeth to remind Bess that it would be her who decided on Arbella's marriage, not Bess.

Arbella certainly had a strong claim to the throne and her biggest asset was that she was born in England, because at this time the law stated that a person had to have been born within the realm in order to have a claim. Sadly, her claim was lacking in support, unlike James, who was becoming over confident and began to get pushy. He even demanded a say in Arbella's marriage negotiations, because he was well aware that if she married an English nobleman then, as a couple, they could amass enough support to oust him from the succession. Elizabeth was keen to remind James that Arbella had just as much of a claim as he did, married or not, and with that warning Arbella was invited to court for the first time. She was aged just 12 when she returned to London but before she could leave Derbyshire she had to be taught how to behave – and what and who to watch out for. No doubt she would have been warned that the queen listened carefully to gossip and had eyes and ears everywhere so Arbella would have been careful what she said and to whom, including Cecil.

Her appearance at court was not just about meeting people, however, it was about making an impression, visually. Bess allowed her granddaughter to have a length of green velvet to make a new gown, but little did Bess – or Arbella – realise that this would go nowhere near close to achieving the required wardrobe for a visit to court. The wardrobes of the greatest ladies could cost more than it cost to run a large estate, but appearances mattered. Arbella was going to see and be seen and Bess knew she would have to make sure her granddaughter looked the part. She dug deep into her extensive funds to provide jewels that would adorn Arbella's dresses and her red Tudor hair, which she would let fall loosely down her back. She would have worn pearls around her neck and a large pendent that would have rested in the middle of her chest.

Arbella's appearances at court would have been eagerly anticipated by many. She had been cossetted away in the Derbyshire countryside for most of her young life, but she was of huge dynastic importance and there was a possibility she would be the next Queen of England. When she was presented to Elizabeth in the presence chamber at Whitehall she would have known how to make the perfect curtsey, keeping her eyes low knowing full well the queen held her whole future completely within her grasp. It has been said that Elizabeth was jealous of Arbella's beautiful long red hair and unblemished fair skin. Arbella's elevated status meant she was given precedence over all the other ladies, she was addressed as your Highness, which no doubt inflated her ego. The education provided by Bess was now coming to the fore as Arbella found herself able to converse with foreign dignitaries and hold intelligent and well-informed conversations with scholars and fellow courtiers which made her appearance at court all the more successful. Arbella had the privilege of dining with the queen and when she was invited to eat with Cecil she met Sir Walter Raleigh who told her stories of his voyages overseas and when he found she was able to converse with him in Spanish the great explorer and statesman was impressed.

It was not long before talk of Arbella's marriage started and Elizabeth was keen to promote a potential match between Arbella and Ranuccio Farnese, the eldest son of the Duke of Palma and Maria of Portugal. But what was Elizabeth's plan? Palma was the Spanish

Governor General of the Netherlands and general of the Spanish army fighting against England. Elizabeth hated war, it was an unnecessary expense as far as she was concerned, and so a political marriage was suggested to stave off the threat of a Spanish attack. Elizabeth had brought Arbella to court to show her off – to put her in the shop window if you will. It was a chance for the foreign ambassadors to see how she looked and behaved and to see if she was queen material. Elizabeth was offering Arbella in the hope of brokering a peace deal, it was quite clear she was nothing more than a political pawn at Elizabeth's disposal.

Arbella left court in August 1588 but stayed in London with her Aunt Mary and Uncle Gilbert, and from her lodgings she often wrote to Bess telling her how well she was doing at court. Her grandmother would have been pleased to learn things were looking good for Arbella. Her strong performance at court encouraged Bess to invest more in her education, looks and finery. The decision was made for her to stay in London a little longer to refine her skills even further. After a while she became an excellent dancer, she took music lessons, read widely and honed all the talents Bess had already taught her. Her patience paid off when she rejoined the court at Greenwich in the summer of 1588 and took an instant liking to the charming Earl of Essex, the new favourite of the queen.

Essex rejected Arbella's attention as he did not want to risk the displeasure of Elizabeth. This upset Arbella, but she was 12 years old and her infatuations came and went. Further rejections came with Farnese and news that the Spanish Armada had been sighted off the Cornish coast. Arbella left London on 13 July, with some speculating that it was because of her childish behaviour towards Essex, some even said it was for her own protection to prevent her from being kidnapped by the Spanish. But in reality the marriage negotiations were off and so she had become surplus to requirements. Arbella was sent back to home to Derbyshire and to Bess, but it is worth noting that out of all of Elizabeth's potential heirs, it was Arbella's position in the European marriage market that was used to help stop the Armada from attacking England and to maintain peace in the country. Elizabeth used Arbella as a pawn, and it is thought a potential marriage with the son of the Duke of Parma, who happened to be the nephew of Philip II of Spain, may have diffused things somewhat.

Life was to change dramatically for Arbella. Gone was the glitz and glamour of the court and in its place came the dullness of Wingfield Manor, consigning her to a lonely and isolated existence. Soon enough she began to rebel, refusing to do her schoolwork; with a feeling of being abandoned and forgotten, who could blame her? When news of Arbella's behaviour reached Bess she decided to take her granddaughter back to Hardwick Hall, but she still remained alone and yearned to be returned to Wingfield Manor, especially when a new tutor was to be installed there to help encourage her back to her books.

In the summer of 1591, Arbella was once again invited back to court, but again it was only in her role as an unwitting peacekeeper – and the marriage with Farnese was back on the table. This time the duke requested to see a likeness of Arbella so the offer of English help must have been an attractive offer to him, and his son. The deal being negotiated was that the English would support him in exchange for a separate principality in the Netherlands over which Ranuccio and Arbella would jointly rule. On this trip to court Arbella was joined by Bess and other members of the family and they resided at Shrewsbury House in Chelsea – this time there was more money to spend on new gowns and jewels because Bess was convinced her granddaughter would one day be queen of England so every penny spent was deemed worth it. As with most marriage negotiations during the Tudor period, religion was a major factor; Farnese was a Catholic and Arbella a Protestant, so in order for a marriage to go ahead she would have to convert to Catholicism. Many tried to convince her this was the right thing to do, because she would gain the support of the English Catholics and those abroad which would have been substantial. But with conversion came risks and she had seen first-hand how religious arguments had destroyed people, Mary, Queen of Scots, was one example.

In October news reached London that a Catholic plot to kidnap Arbella and take her to Flanders and then on to Spain was afoot. The plan seemed to be that once in possession of Arbella, Sir William Stanley, an exiled Catholic living in Spain, would plan to attack England and place her on the throne. Similar plots were made regarding Katherine Grey – the Spanish really wanted to get their hands on England and its crown. As a result, Arbella was sent back to the relative safety of Derbyshire, just in case the plot was successful; the irony was that the Midlands was also a hotbed for Catholic activity. Not long after her return to Derbyshire news came through that the Duke of Palma had died; with him went any chance of a marriage for Arbella. But that did not stop the rumour mill from going into overdrive. Gossip was circulating that she had in fact already married leading Catholic Henry Percy, the future Earl of Northumberland. Where this rumour started and who started it we do not know, but it is unlikely there was any real clout to it. One of the biggest issues facing Arbella's claim was the fact she had no great affiliation with the nobility other than Shrewsbury, which meant no great family links to bankroll her claim. The only way it seemed that she could bolster her chances was through marriage to a well-established noble family. But with Arbella once again isolated in Derbyshire with the aging Bess for company, the chances of that happening were very slim.

When Arbella came of age in 1596 Bess gifted her with land and property which offered her the chance to manage her own household and to receive her own private income – sadly it did not bring her any independence. However, the prospect of a crown and her own income made Arbella a very desirable bride, both at home and in Europe. Although names were still being linked to Arbella, Elizbeth seemed content to let her stagnate in the Derbyshire countryside. One surprising name of a potential groom was Elizabeth's Secretary of State, Robert Cecil. Many believed he wanted to marry Arbella just to become king. He was power hungry and marriage to the heir to the crown seemed like a good idea. Unfortunately for Cecil the thought repulsed Arbella, and also the queen.

Arbella's former crush, the Earl of Essex, was to fall from favour rather spectacularly following the truce he made in Ireland with the Earl of Tyrone. He had made peace against orders, but then abandoned his post and made his way home back to London. When he arrived at court he barged his way into the queen's bedchamber while she was in a state of undress, this was unforgiveable and he was immediately placed under arrest at York House. Essex knew Cecil hated him so he tried to raise the people of London against Cecil and the corrupt government; he failed and was sent to the Tower on a charge of treason. On 1 February 1601, he was found guilty and was executed on 25 February.

Essex was a popular man and Cecil and the queen were heavily criticised for his downfall. It was now clear that Cecil was in charge, but his unpopularity saved Arbella from a marriage to him. Cecil put his backing for the throne behind James, while Arbella was left at home with no company of her own age and rank and with very little family support. She must have felt desperate, alone and forgotten about. But was that Elizabeth's plan all along? We know she had form for leaving her potential heirs ostracised under house arrest, was she doing the same with Arbella? It would certainly seem that way. In fact it seems that she planned to pass her crown to James all along and this was the only way she could deal with Arbella. All Arbella wanted was to escape Derbyshire and the tight clutches of Bess. Like other women of her age and rank, she wanted to marry and have children, she wanted a grand estate to call her own, but Elizabeth kept her under her watchful supervision.

Arbella and the chaplain of Hardwick Hall, James Starkey, had found a selection of letters from London-based solicitor Edward Kyrton that discuss a potential marriage between Arbella and Edward Seymour, 1st Earl of Hertford. It is not 100 per cent clear who the intended recipient of the letters was, but we can presume it was Bess. Arbella decided she had been alone for too long and saw this as her opportunity to break free. She made plans with Starkey for him to go to London to see what he could discover. She gave him £75 for his expenses but sadly things did not go to plan. Starkey told Arbella that he would not be returning to Derbyshire for some months. Arbella was not to be deterred and turned to her uncle Henry Cavendish. Together they arranged for a message to be sent directly to the Earl of Hertford in London to establish if he still wanted to marry Arbella. If he did he was to make his way to Mansfield, Henry Cavendish was to provide an escort and was ready to help his niece escape from the clutches of his mother, Bess. Once again the plan failed. Hertford was suspicious and sent Dodderidge, Arbella's messenger, to Cecil who was convinced there was a Catholic plot afoot to remove Elizabeth from her throne. Dodderidge was thrown into prison at Westminster for two weeks where he made a full written confession. Cecil sent the queen's commissioner, Henry Brouncker, to Hardwick to establish the full details behind the supposed marriage proposal. When he questioned Arbella she denied any knowledge of the letters, or that she had wanted to reopen marriage negotiations with Hertford. What Arbella did not have though was the skill to outwit a man like Brouncker and after a week of interrogation she confessed everything. He asked her to write out a full account of what had happened but the account she gave was jumbled and messy. He asked her to redo it, but again her words were mixed up; in the end he wrote it and asked Arbella to sign it. It appeared that Arbella was struggling mentally, she seemed confused and frightened but in the end Brouncker decided there was no plot and that Bess knew nothing about what her son and granddaughter had been up to.

Bess and Arbella both wrote to the queen to apologise for her behaviour, Bess even went as far as pleading with Elizabeth to take Arbella back to court as she had had enough of her sly and sneaky granddaughter. Bess showed no sympathy towards Arbella, knowing all too well what would happen if she married without royal consent. Arbella had tried to be assertive and take control of her own destiny because, let's face it, no one else seemed that interested and Arbella knew that Elizabeth and Bess were content to let her stagnate. Her plan did not work and she was under even more scrutiny after the letters incident than before. She wrote countless letter to Elizabeth and Cecil but they all went unanswered; word had reached court of Arbella's behaviour and the rumour was that she had gone mad. Who could blame her if she had? She was nothing short of a prisoner at Hardwick Hall, she had no companions and certainly no one she could trust.

Arbella did not help her own cause though. She told Bess that she had a lover, a man who was held in high esteem with the queen. Astounded, Bess told her granddaughter to write down all the details, but Arbella refused to name the mystery man. It was a difficult time for Arbella, she was refusing to eat or drink until she received a response from Elizabeth. Disturbed by this latest development, Elizabeth sent Brouncker back to Hardwick to determine the truth of what was happening. After speaking with Arbella, he discovered the mystery man was in fact a complete fabrication of Arbella. This news angered Bess even further and she hurled abuse at her granddaughter, chasing after her as she made her way back to the sanctuary of her bedchamber. The fabrication of the mystery man and the refusal of food and drink were clear attention-seeking strategies on Arbella's part. She was desperate for help and the only person left for her to turn to was her uncle, Henry Cavendish.

Another plan was made with the aim of helping Arbella escape her Hardwick prison. The date was set for 10 March 1603, and another man, Henry Stapleton, was enlisted to help. The plan was that a group of men would go to Ault Hucknall Church near Hardwick, and from the tower they would be able to see when Arbella was outside taking her daily walk. Unfortunately, they were unable to obtain the keys to the tower and so missed their opportunity. Instead, they decided to present themselves at Hardwick Hall claiming Arbella had wanted to see them. Henry managed to see his niece but as they walked in the garden she was refused permission to leave, Henry had no choice but to leave her behind. Bess was once again furious at Arbella's behaviour and turned again to Brouncker. He returned yet again to Hardwick to discuss what had happened. He interviewed Arbella and Henry and all those connected with the kidnap plot. This turned out to be the last straw for Bess, she cut Arbella from her will and decided she wanted her gone from Hardwick Hall. In June 1603 Mary Cavendish took the opportunity to speak with King James regarding Arbella's treatment by Bess during his stay with the Talbots while making his way to London. James wrote to the Earl of Kent:

> For as much as we are desirous to free our cousin the Lady Arbella Stuart from the unpleasant life that she hath led in the house of her grandmother with whose severity and age, she being a young lady, could hardly agree, we have thought it fit for the present to require you as a nobleman of whose wisdom and fidelity we have heard so good report to be contented for some short space to receive her into your house and there to use her in that manner which is fit for her calling, having the rather made choice of you than of any other because we are informed that your nephew is matched with her cousin Germain in which respect she will like better of that place than of a strangers until further order be taken.

Despite there being strong support at court for Arbella, it seems to have been a forgone conclusion that James would inherit the English throne. Not only was he male, he was also Cecil's choice and as leader of the Privy Council, Cecil's orders were to be obeyed. As a princess of royal blood Arbella was expected to attend the funeral of the queen. As the queen's closest living relative, she had been asked by James to perform the role of chief mourner but Arbella bore a grudge and declined. As Elizabeth had shown her no love or support in life, she had no intention of doing her that favour in death. Over 200,000 people turned out for the funeral of Elizabeth I, sad that their much loved queen had died but also relieved at having a new king.

But what became of Arbella Stuart, first cousin of the new king of England? Arbella placed herself on the mercy of James, she claimed she had no desire to be queen and that she would marry whoever he thought was suitable. She left Wrest Park in Bedfordshire and travelled to court to meet her cousin for the first time. The meeting went well; James told she could live where she wished and even Cecil was helpful when it came to organising her finances. At last Arbella was an independent woman. But the death of Elizabeth and estrangement from Bess meant she had no regular income to support herself at court and James seemed reluctant to support her financially. When Queen Anna arrived at court the two ladies became firm friends meaning Arbella was to spend a lot of time in her company, and her position as a high-ranking lady was costly. It is likely Arbella attended the coronation of King James I at Westminster Abbey on 25 July 1603.

Arbella's elevated status did not go down well with many in James's entourage. All of a sudden precedence had to be given to an English princess that no one seemed to know what to do with. Arbella's limited existence in Derbyshire had left her totally unprepared for the court games, which had to be played correctly in order to gain favour. It was her sheltered upbringing that really hampered her ability to settle at court. She often found solace in her books and spent much of her time at her studies; she disliked the bickering, the fancy gowns and the constant preening and being on show – perhaps it is a good thing she never became queen. Thankfully, by the September of 1603 her finances were on their way to being settled which must have brought her some relief. It had been agreed that she would receive a pension of £800 which James increased to £1,000. This was still far too low for Arbella to maintain herself and her household at court and she quickly began to resent her royal cousin for keeping her in such a state of poverty.

James was not popular and in the July of 1603 eight people were arrested in what became known as the 'Bye Plot'. The crux of the plot was to kidnap James with a view to forcing him to ease the persecution of Catholics. Cecil got wind of the plot and soon there was talk of a second, even bigger plot: the 'Main Plot'. The aim of this second plot was to depose James and place Arbella on the throne. Lord Cobham, one of the conspirators, wrote to Arbella telling her of the plans. She forwarded the letter directly to Cecil in a bid to prove her loyalty, this action probably saved her life – or at the very least a lengthy prison sentence. Arbella's selfless act prompted Cecil to head a full investigation and before long the main culprits, including Sir Walter Raleigh, were rounded up, arrested and charged with 'wanting to raise Arbella Stuart to the throne of England'. Arbella did well to distance herself from this as best she could. She knew that Lady Jane Grey and Mary, Queen of Scots, had both lost their heads after finding themselves embroiled in plots that had not been of their making.

Arbella continued to remain in favour with James who was obviously grateful to her for the role she played in foiling the plot against him. It was proof, if he needed it, that Arbella had no designs on his throne. As a thank you she had been given a blank patent for a peerage that she could give out at her discretion. After long debates she bestowed the title on her uncle, Sir William Cavendish, who became Baron Cavendish of Hardwick, although he would later become the first Earl of Devon. This was an act that brought forgiveness from Bess.

The biggest plot against James was the Gunpowder Plot of 1605. The plan was to blow up the Houses of Parliament, killing James and his heir Henry in the process. The Catholic conspirators wanted to place the young Princess Elizabeth on the throne in his place. There is no evidence to suggest Arbella had any involvement in the plot, although she was mentioned as a potential replacement for James.

Bess of Hardwick died on 13 February 1608, she left Arbella the sum of £1,000. At the age of 33, however, Arbella was still living far beyond her means; she was unmarried and inhabited a lonely position at court. She did manage to buy her own property in Blackfriars which gave her the freedom to leave court. In early autumn 1609 Arbella left London and went on her own summer progress to the Midlands, along the way she made many philanthropic gestures. Aside from her ongoing financial complaints Arbella also repeatedly petitioned the king to find her a husband that pleased him, but like Elizabeth he seemed reluctant. It's likely James was worried about any male children she might have, because her son could become a challenge to his throne – especially as he would have been English born. In her frustration Arbella decided to take the matter into her own hands and one man presented himself as leading contender.

William Seymour and Arbella had been friends since meeting in Oxford, it was a deep friendship and they openly enjoyed each other's company. On 2 February 1610, William proposed to Arbella, she accepted immediately and they took part in a betrothal ceremony, which meant they were as good as married. When James heard the news he was furious and demanded they both appear before the council to explain their actions. William was scrutinised and wrote a formal account of the affair. He believed Arbella was free to marry a husband of her own choosing and that James had agreed to it – and to a certain extent this was true. James had told Arbella to marry a good upstanding man of the realm, which is exactly what she had done. William would have been well aware of the fate of his grandfather Edward Seymour, Earl of Hertford, and his bride Lady Katherine Grey; they had been separated and imprisoned when news of their marriage filtered through to Elizabeth, they remained parted until Katherine's death at the age of just 27.

The choice of William Seymour was a strange one. First, the age gap was fairly large, he was 22 and Arbella was 35, but by all accounts he was everything the men at court were not. He was kind and loving and they both enjoyed similar interests. Of course he had his faults, he was weak-willed and indecisive. Shockingly, one rumour that circulated in court was that Arbella was in fact a man, and that was why she had never married and had children – why else would a noblewoman of 35 remain in such a state? Initially James forgave the couple and put everything down to a misunderstanding so both were welcomed back to court, the rumour mill did not stop turning though. On 21 June 1610 William and Arbella met at Greenwich Palace at the dead of night and among the company of witnesses they were legally married, which they did without the king's consent. They both knew the consequences of the actions; they had family history so it does seem like a reckless decision to make. It took two weeks for James to hear of the news and when he did the newlyweds were arrested. William was sent to the Tower and Arbella was sent to Copt Hall in Lambeth, where she was to remain under house arrest under the watchful eye of Sir Thomas Parry. Parry was Comptroller of the Royal Household, Chancellor of the Duchy of Lancaster, and a member of the Privy Council. The warrant read:

> It is thought fit that the Lady Arbella should be restrained of her liberty, and choice is made of you to receive her and lodge her in your house these are therefore to give you notice thereof, and to require you to provide convenient lodging for her to remain under your charge and custody, with one or two of her women to attend her, without access to any other person until His Majesty's pleasure be further known.

All those involved were arrested and imprisoned and held at various locations around London. Despite being under house arrest Arbella would have been kept in comfortable surroundings, and William was lodged with Sir William Wadd, Lieutenant of the Tower. From there he was assigned chambers in St Thomas's Tower, located over Traitors' Gate, but as his health began to suffer he was given more freedom to walk in the fresh air.

James wanted distance between Arbella and William so he made the decision to banish his cousin to Durham and into the care of the elderly bishop. The journey began in March 1611, but Arbella claimed she was too ill to travel so far. She made it as far as Highgate before having to rest. The journey continued on the 21st when the party managed to make it to Barnet. She was still complaining of feeling ill but James saw this as a delaying tactic; he felt she was play acting for sympathy and sent his own doctor to assess Arbella – who declared her unfit to travel. The king decided to allow Arbella a period of rest and recouperation for a month, but at the end of that time it was clear she was still not well enough to be moved and another month was granted for her recovery.

Arbella's aunt Mary Talbot began a plan to help the couple escape to France. She began raising funds and with the help of her servants Arbella managed to reach Tilbury, where a boat was waiting to take her across the Channel to France. They reached Calais three days later. When the boat docked she decided to remain onboard until William arrived. Back in England William had managed to escape from the Tower with the help of servants and friends. He made his way down to the wharf where his friend Edward Rodney was waiting, but due to delays he missed the French ship that was to take him away from England. Bribes had to be made to other sailors to take them to France. While sailing up the Thames they spotted a French ship at anchor, and boarded to ask for assistance. Unfortunately, the French ship did not have the capacity to take them so they returned to Harwich in their own vessel to await better weather.

By the 4 June, William and Rodney had abandoned their plan to sail to Calais and instead made their way to Ostend, arriving early the following morning. From there they travelled to Bruges, where they heard the news that Arbella had been captured and taken back to England. When James learned that William had escaped he was apoplectic with rage, but the newlyweds had been careless about covering their tracks, making it easy for them to be tracked down. Arbella was apprehended on the evening/early morning of the 6/7 June and conveyed back to London, where she sailed up the Thames to the Tower of London; she would never leave the fortress again. On the other hand, William remained at liberty on the Continent and only returned when he heard of Arbella's death. At which point he wrote to King James asking for permission to return home, the request was granted and he received a pardon. Arbella and William's relationship appeared to have been a true love affair and captured the hearts of the English people, who felt that James's treatment of them was harsh. He remained unmoved.

The sad life of Arbella Stuart ended in the Tower on 25 September 1615; while her cause of death is not clear, her post-mortem suggests she died from the effects of starvation and an unhealthy liver. She had never coveted Elizabeth or James's throne, all she really wanted was to live a happy, private life. She did not enjoy the frivolity of court life and was much happier when at her studies with her books. She was buried in Westminster Abbey at night with no ceremony, James did not even afford his cousin a headstone or tomb. His behaviour of her was deplorable.

Arbella was a serious contender for the throne of England but became nothing more than a political pawn when it suited Elizabeth's needs. Her banishment to Derbyshire and subsequent isolation shaped Arbella's life; she longed for love and affection and when it looked like she had achieved that, it was cruelly snatched away from her. If her paternal grandmother Margaret Douglas had lived longer Arbella's life may have taken a different path, but she lost her parents and doting grandmother far too young. Arbella was a vital member of the royal family but it was likely her gender that put the council off supporting her claim. If she had been male then it is almost certain James would have stayed in Scotland. It was clear people were looking to pitch Arbella against James and when the Suffolk claim ended with the deaths of Katherine and Mary Grey the focus really shifted to the Stuarts, although there were others with weaker claims.

Edward Seymour, Lord Beauchamp

Born on 21 September 1561, at the Tower of London, Lord Beauchamp was the eldest son of Lady Katherine Grey and Edward Seymour, 1st Earl of Hertford. But his claim to the throne was thrown into danger when his parents' married without the consent of Elizabeth I. His mother was imprisoned at the time of his birth and he was baptised at the St Peter ad Vincula chapel within the Tower precincts. His claim came down through Katherine but his father was also from noble stock. His father, Edward's grandfather, had been Edward Seymour, the 1st Duke of Somerset and Lord Protector and uncle of Edward VI, executed in 1552. Beauchamp was therefore also related to Queen Jane Seymour, mother of Edward VI.

At the time of Elizabeth I's death and under the will of her father Henry VIII, which followed the line of his younger sister Mary Tudor, Beauchamp was the most senior claimant to the throne followed by Lady Anne Stanley. If the Scottish line was to be followed, then James and Arbella Stuart were his opposition. As we have seen, Arbella and Beauchamp's lives would cross as she would marry his son and heir William in 1610. Given that Elizabeth I had a strong dislike of Lady Katherine Grey, it is highly unlikely she would have agreed to Beauchamp taking her throne and becoming king, she much preferred to go against the will of her father and name James. But let us also make mention of Edward's younger brother Thomas, also born in the Tower of London in 1562/3. He was born after his parents' marriage had been discovered and so could have been considered legitimate and therefore a possible contender. The reality was that if either of the Seymour brothers had rallied enough support they could have provided a serious challenge to James or Arbella as they held the trump cards of being male, Protestant and English born.

Edward had married Honora Rogers in 1572, a marriage his father disapproved of. The couple had six children together, three boys and three girls, although their two youngest daughters died in infancy. Edward Seymour, Lord Beauchamp, died in July 1612.

Beauchamp is an interesting prospect when it came to being king. He was English and a Protestant, he also had a strong claim to the throne through his mother, but in terms of bloodline he was just that little bit further away than James. Elizabeth priority seems to have been the person closest in terms of bloodline, regardless of other factors. Beauchamp's illegitimacy never seemed to have been an issue for him, he still inherited his titles and estates but in reality he never really pushed his claim and was never a person of interest, especially for the likes of Cecil or Elizabeth. His son William went on to become the Duke of Somerset and was a member of Parliament and later the House of Lords, he seemed to flourish at the court of Charles I and was entrusted to be the guardian of his young son, the future Charles II. His second marriage proved much more successful than his first to Arbella. He married Lady Frances Devereux in March 1617, and the couple had eight children together. Again, he never tried to push a claim to the throne, which is no surprise. After some years in the wilderness following the execution of the Lord Protector, the Seymours were happy to live a quiet life.

Infanta Isabella of Spain

A rather peculiar choice you may think, but Isabella Clara Eugenia had a claim to the English throne through her father, Philip II of Spain, who was descended directly from King Edward III via his son John of Gaunt, and his wife Constance of Castille. Many believed their claim to be much stronger than that of the Tudors even though their descent had come down an illegitimate line from John of Gaunt and his third wife Katherine Swynford, the descendants of that marriage had been barred from ever inheriting the throne given that she was his mistress at the time of their children's births. Isabella was the popular Catholic choice once Mary, Queen of Scots, had been executed. Mary had disinherited James and passed on her right to inherit to Philip of Spain. Along with the Pope, Philip was determined to avenge the death of Mary, it was clear James was not interested in the fate of his mother, but Philip was intent in ridding the world of Protestantism. The thought of Philip inheriting his throne frightened James and he was keen to point out that a foreigner could not inherit – forgetting the fact that he too was foreign, having been born in Scotland, not England.

It was not just Isabella's lineage and religion that made her stand out. She was said to be beautiful, wise and pious – all attributes that make a good queen. Isabella had been well educated; her father saw huge value in his daughters and ensured they were brought up understanding their importance in the world, he even delegated some power to Isabella during the final years of his life. She also had money, which was one thing the English were keen on as it meant she would be unlikely to raise taxes or cause too much worry to the exchequer. Philip, however, was not keen; he had grand plans for his eldest daughter and he sought a marriage with Archduke Albert VII of Austria. Together, they became sovereigns of the Spanish Netherlands, which brought them immense power.

Many Jesuits preferred the candidacy of Isabella and they managed to persuade her brother, Philip III of Spain, to support her claim but Isabella and her husband held very little interest in claiming the English throne. In fact, they both decided to support the claim of James and were even willing to offer money and men should the need arise. Isabella was an unlikely claimant and it wasn't a claim the Spanish royal family were looking to exploit. As it turned out, Isabella and Albert ruled over the Spanish Netherlands with huge success, overseeing a Golden Age which saw Isabella become one of Europe's most powerful and influential women. It is telling then that they had very little interest in adding England to their empire, but when James did come to the throne in 1603, he fostered good relations with Spain and its allies. If the Infanta had pressed her claim for the throne, then Europe could have been looking at all-out war. England would have tried to reject any Spanish involvement and France would have hated the idea of England and Spain joining forces; thankfully, this scenario was avoided and Infanta Isabella settled elsewhere.

Chapter Seven

Was James the Right Choice for England?

There is no question that James was best prepared for the role of becoming the King of England. He had ruled in Scotland for thirty-five years. Unlike any of the other contenders, who had very little to no experience of how the English court was run, James was a monarch with vast experience. But during the early years of his reign his attitude to having his own favourites, and for favouring his Scottish nobles, made him unpopular. Courtier Sir Anthony Weldon described James as being a 'slobbering oddball', referring to the claims that his tongue was too big for his mouth which meant he struggled to eat or drink without making a mess of himself. Physically, James was not a commanding figure; unlike his parents who were both close to 6 foot tall, James was supposedly on the shorter side. His stature would not have been helped by weak bowed legs, possibly from having scurvy as a child or, as many suggest, the trauma experienced by his mother while heavily pregnant with him left a lasting physical impression on him. But as the sources are at odds with each other, let us take these physical descriptions with a pinch of salt.

Physical attributes should have no impact on whether or not James was an able ruler. Unlike his predecessor Elizabeth I, James was not as keen to immerse himself in the day to day running of court. Elizabeth liked to be at the head of every decision made, she would take time to consider each application placed in front of her. James, on the other hand, liked to delegate various tasks to different ministers, giving him more time to spend in the saddle on the hunt. The English court were not used to working this way, and nor did they like it. Decisions should be made by the monarch, not a minister or state secretary, and so they were reluctant to implement changes without James's prior approval.

The running of court was changed dramatically. It went from being the court of an English queen, dominated by women, to the court of a Scottish king, dominated by men. The bedchamber all of a sudden became the centre of politics again, whereas in Elizabeth's reign that remained a female only area with no discussion of state business. The problem was that James liked to surround himself in his more private of chambers with his loyal Scottish men, leaving the English feeling alienated. They could not talk politics if they were not even in the room. As time went on the English grew more and more frustrated with their new monarch. Did they ever stop and think they had made a mistake? Did they wish they had backed Arbella, or even Beauchamp?

There were plots to oust James pretty much from the off, the Bye and Main plots both wanted him ousted and replaced with Arbella, but the biggest by far was the Gunpowder Plot of 1605. If Guy Fawkes and his fellow conspirators had been successful in blowing up the Houses of Parliament it would have been cataclysmic in terms of the succession. With James and his heir Henry dead, there would have been no point in turning to the young Charles, he would have to be dealt with in another manner, but the princess Elizabeth was a different matter. She could have been manipulated into marrying a Catholic and, before England knew it, the country would have been rejoined with Rome.

This was one instance where James's did not respond with leniency. All the conspirators were executed, either by shooting or by being hanged, drawn and quartered. But James was far more tolerant than we give him credit for when it came to religion. He did not really mind if his subjects were Catholic, as long as they supported him as king. But that was not enough; the Catholics wanted more and they were willing to sacrifice James and his son for the greater good of the country.

James was politically astute. In Scotland he managed to juggle the anti-royal supremacy Scots Kirk with keeping his people happy and his nobility loyal. He never shied away from facing his opponents; if a problem needed dealing with then he would do so. He might prefer to delegate ordinary business, but when it came to serious state issues he was ready to make the big decision, such as making peace with Spain.

England was in a poor state of affairs when Elizabeth died, the coffers were depleted thanks to the wars with Spain and Ireland and there was widespread famine, drought and plague. Many believed James would bring change; the country needed religious reform, the Catholics initially wanted tolerance but the Puritans did not think the Reformation had gone far enough, thereby forcing the Catholics to adopt a more aggressive stance. As a Protestant, the Puritans thought James would be on their side, but the Catholics believed he would convert – Queen Anna had already done so, and when he made peace with Spain, they were given even more hope. The peace with Spain not only boosted the exchequer but also brought some religious stability as England was no longer under a threat of attack from Catholic Spain. All James ever wanted was to be liked as king. He was keen to please everyone and made promises to both sides but managed to deliver on neither.

James was definitely a lover and not a fighter; he did not like executions and the number during his reign dropped significantly from those of his Tudor counterparts – and he definitely did not like war. A lot of his nobility were Catholic and the European powerhouses of France and Spain were too, so it made sense to him to be tolerant of Catholics. Having said that, he was no pushover either; he followed the letter of the law and insisted on the use of the Common Book of Prayer and any priest that refused was suspended. In a further move for uniformity he sanctioned the new King James Bible.

The Puritans favoured the Genevan Bible but that held anti-monarchical views and was far too radical for James so naturally he wasn't keen on it. The Bishops' Bible, which was the Church of England's response to the Genevan Bible, was the text sanctioned by the Church but was not commonly used across the country. In 1604 the Hampton Court Convention, led by King James, met to resolve the issues regarding the various translations of the Bible that were being used across the country. The result of this convention was the commissioning of a new Bible that James hoped would settle any lingering disputes the Puritans had over the Bishops' and Genevan translations. James gave strict instructions to the translators that the new Bible must be written in English and to ensure the true beliefs of the Christian Church and the hierarchy of the Church of England were at its core. The first authorised version of the *King James Bible* was printed in 1611 and was sent to parish churches across the country. It was used in the Coronation of King Charles III in May 2023.

One of the most important things for a king is to provide heirs that can prolong his dynasty and James did just that. Sadly, his eldest son and heir, the much loved and adored Prince Henry Frederick, died at the age of 18 in 1612 at St James's Palace London. His death brought widespread grief to England and was considered a tragedy, but there was another son, Charles, and he would later become King Charles I. The Princess Elizabeth married Frederick V, Elector Palatine and became Queen of Bohemia. Queen Anna was considered to be a good queen consort who supported James in his bid for peace with Spain. She was an expert in projecting the magnificence of court. She loved fine gowns and even finer jewels which quickly became a headache for the council. She was a good mother who took interest in her royal offspring; when James removed Henry from her care when he was a baby, which was not unusual for the time, she was devastated and the first thing she did when James set off for London was take him back. In England, she was permitted to see Henry whenever she wished. Her relations with the English were much better than with the Scots, she got on well with Cecil and no doubt shared James's ministers' frustrations when he was absent from court, hunting. When James was away it was Anna who remained at court and met with ambassadors and foreign dignitaries on the king's behalf. She attracted visitors from her native Denmark, her family were frequent visitors to England which led to good relations between the two countries. It would appear Queen Anna was invaluable to James, but sadly he did not seem to appreciate everything his queen did for him and before long she would even be supplanted from the king's bed.

When Cecil died in 1612, Robert Carr became James's favourite. Queen Anna despised Carr and this therefore damaged her relationship with James, especially when the rumours began that the two men were having an affair. It was clear that James, perhaps rather like his mother, let his heart rule his head. He had his favourites and his favourites held a lot of power.

James pushed hard for the union between England and Scotland, he felt that he could not be expected to rule two separate nations and that it would make much more sense to unite the two kingdoms under the name of Great Britain, but parliament was not keen on combining both countries. James's idea of one nation caused anger on both sides of the border. The English did not want their wealth being appropriated by Scotland, and Scotland did not want to abide by the same laws as the English, but James wanted the two nations to be united by peace and not war. It would be James's great-granddaughter, Queen Anne, that would finally see the two countries unite under the Act of Union in 1707.

Appendix One

Henry VIII's Last Will & Testament, dated 30 December 1546

Remembering the great benefits given him by Almighty God, and trusting that every Christian who dies in steadfast faith and endeavours, if he have leisure, to do such good deeds and charitable works as Scripture commands, is ordained, by Christ's Passion, to eternal life, Henry VIII. makes such a Will as he trusts shall be acceptable to God, Christ, and the whole company of Heaven, and satisfactory to all godly brethren in Earth. Repenting his old life, and resolved never to return to the like, he humbly bequeaths his soul to God, who in the person of His son redeemed it and for our better remembrance thereof 'left here with us in his Church Militant the consecration and administration of his precious Body and Blood'; and he desires the Blessed Virgin and holy company of Heaven to pray for and with him, while he lives and in the time of his passing hence, that he may after this 'the sooner attain everlasting life'. For himself he would be content that his body should be buried in any place accustomed for Christian folks, but, for the reputation of the dignity to which he has been called, he directs that it shall be laid in the choir of his college of Windesour, midway between the stalls and the high altar, in a tomb now almost finished in which he will also have the bones of his wife, Queen Jane. And there an altar shall be furnished for the saying of daily masses while the world shall endure.

The tombs of Henry VI. and Edward IV. are to be embellished. Upon his death, his executors shall, as soon as possible, cause the service for dead folk to be celebrated at the nearest suitable place, convey his body to Windsor to be buried with ceremonies (described), and distribute 1,000 mks. In alms to the poor '(common beggars, as much as may be, avoided)' with injunctions to pray for his soul. St. George's College in Windsor Castle shall be endowed (if he shall not have already done it) with lands to the yearly value of 600l., and the dean and canons shall, by indenture, undertake:–(1) to find two priests to say mass at the aforesaid altar; (2) to keep yearly four solemn obits at which 10l. shall be distributed in alms; (3) to give thirteen poor men, to be called Poor Knights, each 12d. a day, and yearly a long gown of white cloth &c. (described), one of the thirteen being their governor and having, in addition, 3l. 6s. 8d. yearly; and (4) to cause a sermon to be made every Sunday at Windsor.

As to the succession of the Crown, it shall go to Prince Edward and the heirs of his body. In default, to Henry's children by his present wife, Queen Catharine, or any future wife. In default, to his daughter Mary and the heirs of her body, upon condition that she shall not marry without the written and sealed consent of a majority of the surviving members of the Privy Council appointed by him to his son Prince Edward. In default, to his daughter Elizabeth upon like condition. In default, to the heirs of the body of Lady Frances, eldest daughter of his late sister the French Queen. In default, to those of Lady Elyanore, second daughter of the said French Queen. And in default, to his right heirs. Either Mary or Elizabeth, failing to observe the conditions aforesaid, shall forfeit all right to the succession.

Appoints as executors of this will the Abp. of Canterbury, the Lord Wriothesley, Chancellor of England, the Lord St. John, Great Master of our House, the Earl of Hertford, Great Chamberlain of England, the Lord Russell, Lord Privy Seal, the Viscount Lisle, High Admiral of England, the bishop Tunstall of Duresme, Sir Anthony Broun, Master of our Horse. Sir Edward Montagu, chief judge of the 'Commyn Place,' Justice Bromley. Sir Edward North, Chancellor of the Augmentations, Sir William Paget, our chief Secretary, Sir Anthony Denny and Sir William Harbard, chief gentlemen of our Privy Chamber, Sir Edward Wootton and Dr. Wootton his brother. All these shall also be Councillors of the Privy Council with Prince Edward; and none of them shall do anything appointed by this Will alone, but only with the written consent of the majority. Sir Edmond Peckham, cofferer of our House, shall be treasurer of all moneys defrayed in performance of this Will. Debts, with redress of injuries (if any such can be proved, although he knows of none) shall be their first care after his burial. All grants and recompenses which he has made or promised but not perfected are to be performed.

To his son Edward he gives the succession of his realms of England and Ireland, the title of France and all his dominions, and also all his plate, household stuff, artillery, ordnance, ships, money and jewels, saving such portions as shall satisfy this Will; charging his said son to be ruled as regards marriage and all affairs by the aforesaid Councillors (names repeated) until he has completed his eighteenth year. And the following persons shall be of Council for the assistance of the foresaid Councillors when required, viz., the present earls of Arundel and Essex, Sir Thomas Cheney, treasurer of our Household, Sir John Gage, comptroller of our Household, Sir Anthony Wingfield, our vice-chamberlain, Sir William Petre, one of our two principal secretaries, Sir Richard Riche, Sir John Baker, Sir Ralph Sadleyr, Sir Thomas Seymour, Sir Richard Southwell, and Sir Edmond Peckham.

Bequeaths to his daughters', Mary and Elizabeth's, marriages to any outward potentate, 10,000l. each, in money, plate, etc., or more at his said executors' discretion; and, meanwhile, from the hour of his death, each shall have 3,000l. to live upon, at the ordering of ministers to be appointed by the foresaid Councillors.

The Queen his wife shall have 3,000l. in plate, jewels and stuff, besides what she shall please to take of what she has already, and further receive in money 1,000l. besides the enjoyment of her jointure.

For their kindness and good service his executors shall receive as follows, :–the Abp. of Canterbury 500 mks., Wriothesley, St. John, Russell, Hertford and Lisle, each 500l., Durham, Broun, Paget, Denny, Herberd, Montague, Bromley, North, Sir Edw. Wootton and Dr. Wootton, each 300l.

In token of special love and favour, these Councillors and servants shall receive as follows, viz.:–The earl of Essex, Sir Thomas Cheney, the Lord Herberd, Sir John Gage, Sir Thomas Seymour, John Gates and Sir Thomas Darcy, each 200l., Sir Thomas Speke, Sir Philip Hobby, Sir Thomas Paston and Sir Maurice Barkeley, each 200 mks., Sir Ralph Sadleyr 200l., Sir Thomas Carden 200l., Sir Peter Meutes, Edward Bellingham, Thomas Audeley and Edmond Harman, each 200 marks, John Pen 100 marks, Henry Nevel, Symbarbe, — Cooke, John Osburn and David Vincent, each 100l., James Rufforth, keeper of our house here, — Cecil, yeoman of our Robes, — Sternhold, groom of our Robes, each 100 mks., John Rouland, page of our Robes, 50l., the earl of Arundell, Lord Chamberlain, Sir Anthony Wingfeld, Sir Edm. Peckham, Sir Richard Riche, Sir John Bak[er] and Sir Richard Southwell, each 200l., Dr. Owen, Dr. Wendy and Dr. Cromer, each 100l., — Alsopp, Patrick —, —A[yliff], — Ferrys, Henry—, and — Hollande. each 100 mks., and the four gentlemen ushers of our Chamber, being daily waiters, 200l.

His executors may appoint legacies to other of his ordinary servants not here named.

Westminster Palace, 30 Dec. 1546, 38 Hen. VIII. Signed with the King's stamp at beginning and end.

Signed by witnesses, viz.: John Gates: E. Harman: Wyllyam Sayntbarbe: Henry Nevell: Rychard Coke: David Vincent: Patrec: [Ge]orge Owen: [Tho]mas Wendye: Robert Huycke: W. Clerk.

Extract taken from the following link Henry VIII: December 1546, 26-31 | British History Online (british-history.ac.uk)

Appendix Two

The Golden Speech

The Golden Speech given by Elizabeth I on 30 November 1601 in the Palace Council Chamber to 141 members of the Commons including The Speaker. The speech addresses the economic state of the country at that time and give some indication as to the state of England at the time James ascended the English throne in 1603.

Her Majesties most Princelie answere, delivered byher selfe at the Court of Whitehall, on the last day of November 1601: When the Speaker of the Lower House of Parliament (assisted with the greatest part of the Knights, and Burgesses) had presented their humble thanks for her free and gracious favour, in preventing and reforming of sundry grievances, by abuse of many Grants, commonly called Monopolies. The same being taken verbatim in writing by A.B. [possibly Anthony Blagrave] as neere as he could possibly set it downe.

Mr Speaker, we perceive by you, whome we did constitute the mouth of our Lower House, howe with even consent they are fallen into the due consideration of the precious gift of thankefulnesse, most usually least esteemed, where it is best deserved. And therefore we charge you tell them how acceptable such sacrifice is woorthily received of a loving King, who doubteth much whether the given thanks can be of more poise [i.e. weight] then the owed is to them: and suppose that they have done more for us, then they themselves beleeve. And this is our reason: Who keepes their Sovereigne from the lapse of error, in which, by ignorance, and not by intent, they might have fallen; what thankes they deserve, we know, though you may gesse. And as northing is more deere unto us then the loving conservation of our subjects hearts, what an undeserved doubt might we have incurred, if the abusers of our liberality, the thrallers of our people, the wringers of the poore, had not bene tolde us! Which, ere our heart or hand should agree unto, we wish we had neither: and do thanke you the more, supposing that such griefes touch not some among you in particular. We trust there resides, in their conceits of us, no such simple cares of their good, whome we so deerly prize, that our hand should passe ought that might injure any, though they doubt not it is lawfull for our kingly state to grant gifts of sundry sorts of whom we make election, either for service done, or merit to be deserved, as being for a King to make choise on whom to bestow benefits, more to one then another. You must not beguile your selves, nor wrong us, to thinke that the glosing lustre of a glistring glory of a Kings title may so extoll us, that we thinke all is lawfull what we list, not caring what we doe: Lord, how farre should you be off from our conceits! For our part we vow unto you, that we suppose Physicians aromaticall favours, which in the top of their potion they deceive the Patient with, or gilded drugges that they cover their bitter sweet with, are not more beguilers of senses, then the vanting [vaunting] boast of a kingly name may deceive the ignorant of such an office. I grant, that such a Prince as cares but for the dignity, nor passes not how the raines be guided, so he rule, to such a one it may seeme an easie businesse. But you are cumbred (I dare assure) with no such Prince, but such a one, as lookes how to give account afore another Tribunal seat then this world affords, and that hopes, that if wee discharge with conscience what he biddes, will not lay to our charge the fault that our Substitutes (not being our crime) fall in. We thinke our selves most fortunately borne under such a starre, as we have bene inabled by Gods power to have saved you under our reigne, from forreigne foes, from Tyrants rule, and from your owne ruine; and doe confesse, that wee passe not so much to be a Queene, as to be a Queene of such Subjects, for whom (God is witnesse, without boast or vaunt) wee would willingly lose our life, ere see such to perish. I blesse God, he hath given me never this fault of feare; for he knowes best, whether ever feare possest me, for all my dangers: I know it is his gift; and not to hide his glory, I say it. For were it not for conscience, and for your sake, I would willingly yeeld another my place, so great is my pride in reigning, as she that wisheth no longer to be, then Best and Most would have me so. You know our presence can not assist each action, but must distribute in sundrie sorts to divers kindes our commands. If they (as the greatest number bee commonly the woorst) shoulde (as I doubt not but some doe) abuse their charge, annoy whom they should helpe, and dishonour their king, whom they should serve: yet we verely beleeve, thatall you will (in your best judgement) discharge us from such guilts. Thus we commend us to your constant faith, and your selves to your best fortunes.

Extract taken from the following link The Golden Speech – The National Archives

Appendix Three

The Treaty of Edinburgh 1560

The Treaty of Edinburgh dated 6 July 1560 between Queen Elizabeth of England, King Francois II of France and Mary, Queen of Scots.

Articles I and II: [The treaty of Cambray is confirmed].

III, It is appointed, agreed, and concluded, That all the military forces pertaining to either party by sea or land, shall depart out of Scotland, after the manner, and upon the terms, as mail be agreed by particular articles, signed and sealed by the respective commissioners; such a certain number of French soldiers excepted, as shall be condescended upon by the commissioners of France, and the lords of Scotland, to remain in the castle of Dunbar, and fort of Inch-keith.

IV, It is appointed, agreed, and concluded, That all manner of warlike preparations in England and Ireland against the French or Scots; and in France against the English, Irish, or Scots, shall hereafter cease: So that no ships having on board any soldiers or warlike instruments, or preparations for war, shall be allowed to pass from England or Ireland, or from any other part, into France or Scotland, by and with the consent of Elizabeth queen of England; nor from France, nor any other part, to England, Ireland, or Scotland, by and with the consent of Francois and Mary king and queen of France and Scotland.

V, Seeing in the forementioned treaty of Cambray, it was agreed and concluded, That the fort built at Aymouth in the kingdom of Scotland, should have been demolished within three months after the date of the said treaty, razed to the ground, and nothing ever thereafter to have been built there: And although the said fort be in some sort demolished, yet not so as was agreed upon; therefore it is now appointed, agreed, and concluded, That the said fort of Aymouth shall be utterly demolished and razed before the end of four days, after the demolition of Leith shall begin. And in the demolishing of the said fort, such Scottish men as shall be deputed thereunto by the commissioners, shall be at freedom to make use of the labour of English pioneers.

VI, Seeing the kingdoms of England and Ireland do, by right, pertain to the most serene lady and princess Elizabeth; upon which account it is not lawful for any other persons to call, write, name, or entitle themselves, nor yet to order themselves to be called, written, named, or entitled king and queen of England or Ireland, nor to use or take to themselves the ensign's armorial, or arms of the kingdom of England or Ireland: Therefore it is appointed, agreed, and concluded, That the said most Christian king and Queen Mary, and both of them, shall in all times coming, abstain from using and bearing the said title and arms of the kingdom of England or Ireland, and shall strictly prohibit and forbid their subjects in France and Scotland, and the provinces thereof, from using the said title and arms any manner of way; and shall likewise prohibit and take care, so far as in them lies, that no person quarter the said ensigns armorial with the arms of the kingdoms of France or Scotland. And if there be any public letters or writings which carry in them the title of the kingdoms of England or Ireland, or be sealed with the seal of the said kingdoms, or either of them; the fame shall be renewed, without the abjection of the title and arms of England and Ireland; and all letters and writings containing the said title, or sealed with the seals of the said arms, which shall not be renewed within six months after the publication of this present treaty, shall be void, and of no avail. Finally, they shall take care, so far as they can, that in the said kingdoms of France and Scotland, the said arms be no where extant, seen, or found mixed with the arms of the said king or Queen Mary; and that the said title be no where extant, seen or found ascribed to the said king or Queen Mary.

VII, Whereas the commissioners of the most serene Queen Elizabeth did require, that the foregoing caution and provision contained in the close of the article immediately proceeding, should be published by open proclamation; and did likewise insist on a further compensation and reparation for the injuries which they alleged were done to the said most serene Queen Elizabeth, by the said most serene king and Queen Mary: And whereas the commissioners of France, after having replied sundry things in answer thereunto, did farther add, that they had no authority to treat or conclude any thing concerning these particulars; and if they should wait until a return shall come from France, not only would there arise from thence a great loss of time; but moreover strong impediments may come in the way of completing the present treaty of peace and amity: therefore it is appointed, agreed and concluded, that the disceptation concerning the above demands, namely, concerning the publication of the foresaid caution, and concerning a farther reparation, shall be remitted to another meeting at London between the said commissioners of both parties, to be assembled as quickly as conveniently may be. And if nothing can be got concluded, concerning the said disceptation, before the end of three months, to be reckoned from the date of the present treaty 5 in that case, the said disceptation shall, by consent of both parties, be referred to the arbitration of the most mighty prince Philip the Catholic King of Spain, to whose sentence and award both parties shall stand. And if the said Catholic King shall not find it convenient for him to pronounce a final decree in writing, concerning these matters, within a year after the aforesaid three months are elapsed, excepting still if the term shall not chance to be prolonged by consent of both parties; whether there be no such prolongation of the time, or the said Catholic King do not put an end to the said disceptation within the time so prolonged: in either of these cases, the said most serene Queen Elizabeth's right of suing for these things shall be reserved entire to her, in the same state and condition it was in before the commencement of this treaty.

VIII, Seeing it hath pleased Almighty God, in whose hands are the hearts of kings, so to incline the minds of the said most Christian king and Queen Mary, that they have largely manifested their clemency and benignity towards their nobility and people of their kingdom of Scotland, and that reciprocally the said nobility and people have willingly, and of their own accord, acknowledged, professed, and promised all duty and obedience to the said most Christian king and queen their sovereigns: For the better preservation, cherishing, and continuance whereof, the said most Christian king and queen have, by their said commissioners, granted their assent to certain supplicatory petitions presented by the said nobility and people to the said king and queen, tending to the honour of the said king and queen, to the public benefit of the said kingdom, and to the continuation of their obedience. And the said most Christian king and queen being desirous to have their said benignity towards their said subjects attributed to the good offices of the (aid. most serene Queen Elizabeth, their most dear sister and confederate, at whose intercession and request the said king and queen have been more propensity moved hereunto; therefore it is agreed between the foresaid commissioners of both parties, That the said most Christian king and Queen Mary shall fulfil all those things which, by their said commissioners, they have granted to the said nobility and people of Scotland at Edinburgh the sixth Day of July, in this present year 1560, provided the said nobility and people of Scotland shall fulfil and observe all those things that are contained in the said articles and conventions to tie performed on their part.

IX, In this treaty of peace and amity is comprehended, on the part of the said most serene princes Francis the most Christian king of France and Queen Mary, as likewise on the part of the most serene Elizabeth queen of England, the most potent prince Philip the Catholic king of Spain, conformable to the force and effect of treaties subsisting between the said kings and queens, their kingdoms, territories, countries, and dominions.

X, It is appointed, agreed, and concluded, That this present treaty, with all, and several, the conventions and contents thereof, shall be ratified and confirmed by the said most mighty and illustrious Francis and Mary, and Elizabeth, and each of them, within the space of sixty days after the date of this treaty, and shall be turned by them into letters patents, with their great seals appended, and their proper manual subscriptions adjoined: And the said princes, and each of them shall deliver the said confirmatory authentic letters, so subscribed and sealed, to the commissioner or commissioners of the other prince, having authority to this effect.

XI, It is appointed, agreed, and concluded, That the said most illustrious and most mighty princes, Francis and Mary, and Elizabeth, and every of them, shall in the presence of the commissioner or commissioners of the other prince, having sufficient authority for this effect, if required by him or them, promise on their royal word, and swear upon God's holy gospel; and every of them shall so swear, that they shall truly, inviolably, and in good faith, observe, for their part, all, and every, the articles, conventions, provisions, and facts, comprehended in this present league and treaty.

Here follows the tenon of the commissions
In faith and testimony of all which and singular the premisses, we the aforesaid commissioners and ambassadors have caused these letters patents subscribed with our hands, to be fortified and corroborated by our seals.

These things were done at Edinburgh within the said kingdom of Scotland, the 6th day of July, 1560.

This transcript was taken from WikiSources on Tuesday 23rd July 2024.

Appendix Four

James I speech in the Banqueting Chamber on 21 March 1610 on Divine Right of Kings

Although this time of Lent be a time of restraint and penitence, yet since these 2 days have been so well spent giving thanks, I will now make up the terminal [final] number which is the most present to make this Eucharistical thanks giving the more complete to add mine also to the service.

And now I must remember you of that I always and often but formerly wished that the King's heart were a Crystal glass that you might truly see it, it is said that *cor regis est in meum dominum* [the king's heart is in the hand of the Lord], but I wish how that *cor regis* should be *in oculis populi* [the King's heart should be in the eyes of the people], and this is but reminiscentia [reminiscent] of things I have often here to for spoken etc.

There be 3 things have been spoken of this Parliament.

The cause why the Parliament was called

The complaints and grievances of the people

An accident by chance fallen in & yet of an high nature, as what form of government the King should use whether he will establish the laws & govern by them, or alter them, or bring in some new laws.

But he doth protest he is utterly against any such courses, & therefore he will cry down Cowell's book and all the matters of that nature, & will have all men know that he hath been as little carried away with flatterers which make kings omnipotent as ever was any and this was never his fault.

He must say somewhat to the sermon preached on Sunday was sought because it is so much talked of & he thought the preacher preached nothing but truth but if I (saith the King) had been in his place I would have had the discretion to have said somewhat more, all I suppose he would if the time had proved, for all he said was true divinity in a King generally but not in every particular King.

And now because every Christian is bound to give an account of his faith I will hold it my duty to let my people know what I hold in this point.

Kings are gods on earth & this is illustrated by 3 degrees of comparison….

Bibliography

Armitage, J. *Arbella Stuart: The Uncrowned Queen*, (Amberley Publishing, Stroud, 2019)

Armitage, J, *Four Queens and a Countess*, (Amberley, Stroud, 2019)

Borman, T. *Elizabeth's Women: The Hidden Story of the Virgin Queen*, (Vintage, London, 2010)

Byrne, C. *Lady Katherine Grey: A Dynastic Tragedy*, (The History Press, Cheltenham, 2023)

Clarke, S & Collins, L, *Gloriana: Elizabeth & the Art of Queenship*, (The History Press, Cheltenham, 2022)

Clegg, M, *Margaret Tudor: The Life of Henry VIII's Sister*, (Pen and Sword History, Barnsley, 2018)

De Lisle, L. *Tudor: The Family Story* (Chatto and Windus, London, 2013)

De Lisle, L. *After Elizabeth: The Death of Elizabeth and the Coming of King James,* (Harper Press, 2006, London)

Durant, D.N., *Bess of Hardwick: A Portrait of an Elizabethan Dynasty*, (Peter Owen Publishers, London, 2008)

Gristwood, S. *England's Lost Queen Arbella*, (Bantam Books, London, 2004)

Gristwood, S. *Game of Queens: The Women Who Made Sixteenth-Century Europe*, (Oneworld, London, 2016)

Guy, J. *Elizabeth: The Forgotten Years*, (Viking, London, 2016)

Guy, J. *My Heart is My Own: The Life of Mary Queen of Scots*, (Fourth Estate, London, 2009)

Hilton, L. *Elizabeth: Renaissance Prince, A Biography*, (Weidenfeld & Nicholson, London, 2015)

Lipscomb, S. *The King is Dead: The Last Will and Testament of Henry VIII*, (Head of Zeus, London 2015)

Licence, Amy. *Tudor Roses: From Margaret Beaufort to Elizabeth I,* (Amberley Publishing, Stoud, 2022)

McGregor, M. *The Other Tudor Princess*, (The History Press, Stroud, 2016)

Ring, M. *So High a Blood*, (Bloomsbury, London, 2018)

Skidmore, C. *Death and the Virgin: Elizabeth, Dudley and the Mysterious Fate of Amy Robsart*, (Weidenfeld & Nicolson, London, 2010)

Spencer, C. *The White Ship: Conquest, Anarchy and the Wrecking of Henry I's Dream*, (William Collins, London, 2021)

Somerset, A. *Elizabeth I*, (Phoenix, London, 1997)

Stedall, R. *Mary Queen of Scots' Downfall: The Life and Murder of Henry, Lord Darnley*, (Pen and Sword History, Barnsley, 2017)

Tallis, N. *Elizabeth's Rival: The Tumultuous Life of Lettice Knollys, Countess of Leicester*, (Michael O'Mara Books, London, 2018)

Weir, A. *Henry VIII: King and Court*, (Vintage, London, 2010)

Weir, A. *The Lost Princess: A Life of Margaret Douglas, Countess of Lennox*, (Jonathan Cape, London, 2015)

Whitelock, A. *Mary Tudor: England's First Queen*. (Bloomsbury Publishing, London. 2010)

Whitelock, A. *Elizabeth's Bedfellows: An Intimate History of the Queen's Court,* (Bloomsbury, London, 2013)

Wooding, L. *Tudor England: A History*, (Yale University Press, London, 2022)

Index